REVISE BTEC

Applied Science
Principles of Applied Science
UNIT 1
REVISION GUIDE

Series Consultant: Harry Smith   Author: Jennifer Stafford-Brown

THE REVISE BTEC SERIES

Applied Science Principles of Applied Science Revision Guide   9781446902776

Applied Science Principles of Applied Science Revision Workbook   9781446902783

Applied Science Application of Science Revision Guide   9781446902837

Applied Science Application of Science Revision Workbook   9781446902844

This Revision Guide is designed to complement your classroom and home learning, and to help prepare you for the external test. It does not include all the content and skills needed for the complete course. It is designed to work in combination with Edexcel's main BTEC Applied Science 2012 Series.

To find out more visit:
www.pearsonschools.co.uk/BTECsciencerevision

ALWAYS LEARNING   **PEARSON**

Contents

A small bit of small print
Edexcel publishes Sample Assessment Material and the Specification on it website. This is the official content and this book should be used in conjunction with it. The questions in *Now try this* have been written to help you practise every topic in the book. Remember: the real exam questions may not look like this.

Cell structure and function 1

Different types of cell have different structures as they have different functions to perform. Below are four examples of SPECIALISED animal cells and how they are ADAPTED to carry out their function.

1 White blood cell

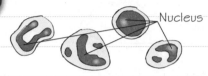
Nucleus

- FUNCTION – protects the body from infection.
- STRUCTURE – can change shape easily, which allows them to squeeze through the walls of blood vessels to get to infected tissues.

2 Red blood cell

This is a cross-section view of a red blood cell

- FUNCTION – contains haemoglobin to carry oxygen, which is transported in the blood.
- STRUCTURE – has no nucleus. One reason for this is that it increases the amount of space inside the cell for haemoglobin.

3 Motor neurone

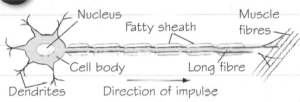
Nucleus — Fatty sheath — Muscle fibres
Cell body — Long fibre
Dendrites — Direction of impulse

- FUNCTION – motor neurones transmit electrical impulses from the central nervous system to muscles and organs.

4 Sensory neurone

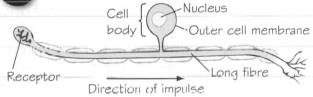
Cell body { — Nucleus — Outer cell membrane
Receptor — Long fibre
Direction of impulse

- FUNCTION – sensory neurones transmit electrical impulses from sense organs such as the eyes and ears to the central nervous system.

- STRUCTURE – a single neurone has a very long fibre, which enables lots of neurones with long fibres linked together to connect your brain to muscles in your toes. It also has branches at the end, called dendrites, which connect to many other cells.

Worked example

(a) Describe the function of a sensory neurone. **(1 mark)**
To carry signals from sense organs to the brain.
(b) Explain how a neurone is adapted to its function. **(2 marks)**
Many branched endings so the signal can be passed on to many cells.

> Make sure you describe the structure and also say **why** this structure makes the cell suited to do its job.

Now try this

1 How is the structure of red blood cells suited to their function? **(1 mark)**
  - A ☐ They have a large surface area to carry oxygen
  - B ☐ They can change shape to allow them to engulf bacteria
  - C ☐ They contain lots of cytoplasm to carry food to other cells
  - D ☐ They have a streamlined shape for swimming through the blood

2 Describe the function of a motor neurone. **(1 mark)**

1

Cell structure and function 2

Plants cells often have different functions from animal cells, so they adapt in different ways.

Animal cells

1 Egg cell

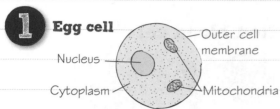

Outer cell membrane
Nucleus
Cytoplasm
Mitochondria

- FUNCTION – to join with the sperm cell.
- STRUCTURE – it is a very large cell so that it can provide food for the fertilised egg.

2 Sperm cell

Mitochondria
Nucleus
Cytoplasm
Tail
Head

- FUNCTION – to fertilise an egg cell.
- STRUCTURE – the head contains genetic material and the tail helps it swim to the egg.

Plant cells

3 Root hair cell

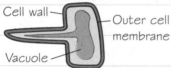

Cell wall
Outer cell membrane
Vacuole

- FUNCTION – to absorb water and minerals from the soil.
- STRUCTURE – the long extension gives it a large surface area, which allows the cell to absorb more water.

4 Xylem and phloem cells

- FUNCTION – xylem allows the transport of water around the plant and also provides support. Phloem transports sugars from the leaves around the rest of the plant.
- STRUCTURE – both these types of cell join together to make continuous tubes. Xylem cells also have a hard wall which helps support the weight of the plant.

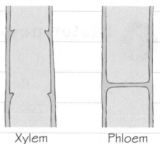

Xylem   Phloem

Worked example

The diagram opposite shows **guard cells** on a leaf. The guard cells are shown at two different times. Explain how guard cells are adapted to help the leaf photosynthesise.   **(2 marks)**

By changing from a curved to a straight shape or back again, guard cells can open or close a pore or small hole (a stoma) in the leaf. When the guard cells open the pore, this lets carbon dioxide in, which is needed for photosynthesis.

Curved guard cells   Straight guard cells

The diagram gives you a hint as to what the function of guard cells is. You have to give a reason how this helps the leaf to photosynthesise.

Now try this

1 Describe the structure and function of a sperm cell.   **(3 marks)**

2 What is the function of:
   (a) xylem cells?   **(2 marks)**
   (b) phloem cells?   **(1 mark)**

You should give **two** functions of xylem cells.

Plant cell organelles

An organelle is a specialised structure within a cell that is adapted to perform a specific function. Plants can make their own food using sunlight in a process called PHOTOSYNTHESIS. Plant cells contain organelles that are specialised to carry out this process.

CELL MEMBRANE
Controls how substances enter and leave the cell.

NUCLEUS
Contains genetic information that controls the activities of the cell.

CELL WALL
Provides shape and strength to the cell.

VACUOLE
Filled with cell sap which stores nutrients; the sap also provides extra support for the cell.

MITOCHONDRIA
Where respiration takes place.

CHLOROPLASTS
Where photosynthesis takes place.

CYTOPLASM
Where many chemical reactions essential for life take place.

A plant cell can have many chloroplasts and many mitochondria, but only one nucleus.

You need to remember that respiration reactions and photosynthesis reactions do **not** take place in the cytoplasm.

Worked example

Explain why a plant cell usually has a regular shape.
(2 marks)

A plant cell has a rigid cell wall surrounding it, which helps to give the cell a rectangular shape.

To answer an explain question you need to describe a feature **and** explain what this feature does.

Now try this

1 The diagram shows a plant cell.
   (a) Name cell part A.   **(1 mark)**
   (b) Describe the function of cell part A.   **(1 mark)**
   (c) Name cell part B.   **(1 mark)**
   (d) Describe the function of cell part B.   **(1 mark)**

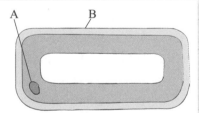

Make sure you spell words such as chloroplast, cytoplasm, mitochondria and vacuole correctly.

Animal cell organelles

Animal cells do not have as many organelles, or components, as plant cells. You need to know which components they do contain.

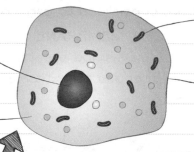

NUCLEUS
Contains genetic information that controls the activities of the cell.

CYTOPLASM
Where many chemical reactions essential for life take place.

MITOCHONDRIA
Where respiration takes place.

CELL MEMBRANE
Controls how substances enter and leave the cell.

Animal cells are usually an irregular shape, because they do not have a rigid cell wall.

Comparing animal and plant cells

Component	Plant cell	Animal cell
Nucleus	✓	✓
Cell membrane	✓	✓
Cell wall	✓	✗
Cytoplasm	✓	✓
Vacuole	✓	✗
Chloroplast	✓	✗
Mitochondria	✓	✓

Worked example

Describe the functions of the following components of a cell.

(a) Nucleus. **(2 marks)**

Contains genetic information which controls the activities of a cell.

(b) Cell membrane. **(1 mark)**

Controls what goes into and out of a cell.

(c) Cytoplasm. **(1 mark)**

Many chemical reactions occur here.

Now try this

1 Which **one** of the following structures is found in both a plant and an animal cell? **(1 mark)**

   A ☐ chloroplast

   B ☐ vacuole

   C ☐ nucleus

   D ☐ cell wall

You need to know that plant cells have some parts that animal cells do not.

2 Which of the following structures is generally found only in a plant cell? **(1 mark)**

   A ☐ nucleus

   B ☐ chloroplast

   C ☐ cell membrane

   D ☐ cytoplasm

3 Explain why an animal cell is usually an irregular shape. **(2 marks)**

Cells, tissues and organs

Specialised cells with similar structures and functions are joined together to make a TISSUE. Different tissues are then joined up to make an ORGAN. An ORGAN SYSTEM is a group of organs that work together to carry out a particular function in the body.

cells → tissues → organs → organ system

The heart as an example

The heart is an organ that contains many cell types and many different tissues.

Muscle cells are specialised to contract and relax

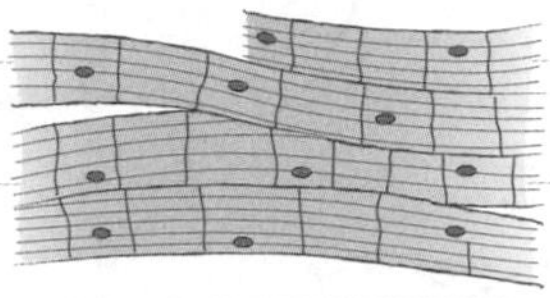

Muscle cells are joined together to make muscle tissue

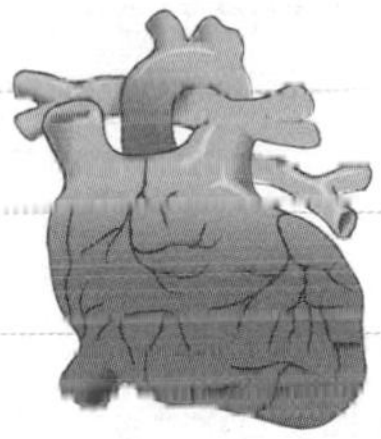

Groups of different tissues are joined together to make the heart

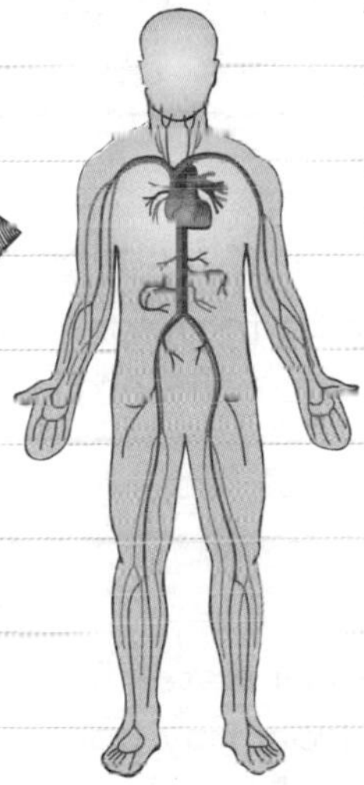

The heart and blood vessels work together to circulate blood around the body

You should be able to use the circulation system (also called the **cardiovascular system**) as an example to identify one organ, one tissue and one cell type.

Organs

Organs perform a specific function in animals or plants. Other examples of human organs include:

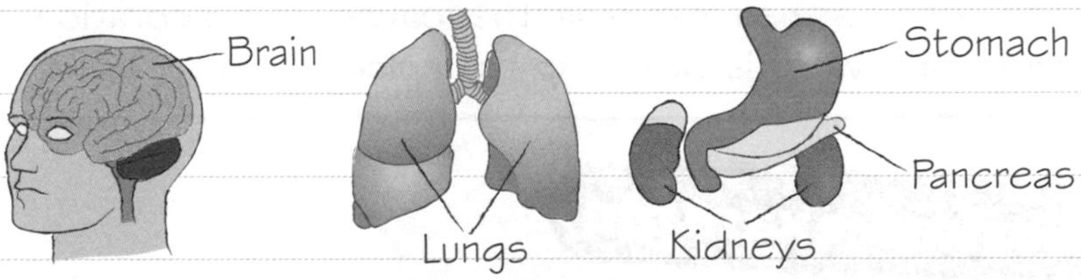

Brain

Stomach

Pancreas

Lungs

Kidneys

Worked example

Which organ is part of the cardiovascular system? **(1 mark)**

A ☐ liver

B ☐ brain

C ☐ small intestine

D ☒ heart

Now try this

1 Which **one** of the following is an example of a cell? **(1 mark)**

A ☐ motor neurone   B ☐ nucleus

C ☐ flower   D ☐ heart

2 Which **one** of the following is an example of an organ? **(1 mark)**

A ☐ mitochondria   B ☐ vacuole

C ☐ liver   D ☐ chloroplast

Function of plant organs

Plants have a number of different organs and tissues, and each has a specific function to help the plant to grow and stay alive.

cells ➡ tissues ➡ plant organs

LEAF
This is where photosynthesis takes place to make food for the plant.

ROOTS
Take in water and minerals from the soil and provide anchorage.

XYLEM
This tissue carries water and mineral salts from the roots to every part of the plant.

This is a cross-section of the stem

PHLOEM
This tissue carries glucose made by the leaves to other parts of the plant.

Tissues

Specialised cells with the same function are grouped together to form tissues.

Xylem cells group together to form long tubes through the plant, so we call the tubes xylem tissue. Similarly, phloem cells group together to form long tubes or phloem tissue.

Transpiration

TRANSPIRATION is the loss of water from leaves. Leaves lose water by evaporation from tiny pores (stomata) in the leaf. This draws water up from the roots to every part of the plant through the xylem tissue.

The water is then lost from the leaves via evaporation and more water is drawn up to replace this lost water.

Water lost by evaporation from pores in leaves

Xylem tissue in roots and stem carries water upwards

Water absorbed by root hairs

Transpiration

Worked example

Name the specialised cell in leaves which controls transpiration.

(1 mark)

Guard cell.

You need to link together your knowledge of specialised cells in plants (see page 2 for more information) with your knowledge of transpiration.

Now try this

1   Name the plant tissue that:
   (a) carries water through the plant   **(b)** carries glucose through the plant.

(2 marks)

DNA

DNA stands for Deoxyribonucleic Acid. It is found in the nucleus of every cell and carries the genetic instructions for making living organisms.

DNA structure

DNA is a very long molecule made up of four different BASES arranged in sequences on two strands.

The four bases are, ADENINE (A), THYMINE (T), GUANINE (G) and CYTOSINE (C).

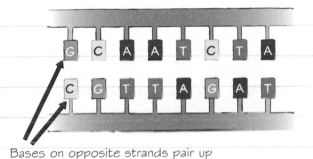

Bases on opposite strands pair up

Base pairs

Adenine always pairs with thymine: A–T

Guanine always pairs with cytosine: G–C

These are called COMPLEMENTARY BASE PAIRS.

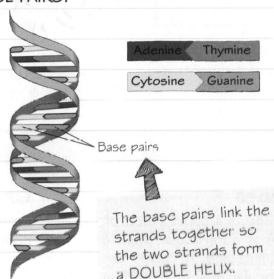

Base pairs

The base pairs link the strands together so the two strands form a DOUBLE HELIX.

Worked example

One strand of a DNA molecule consists of the following sequence of bases:

    A   C   A   G   T

Write down the sequence of bases on the complementary strand.   **(1 mark)**

    T   G   T   C   A

You need to remember the rules for how the bases pair up:

    A–T
    G–C

A mnemonic might help you remember (All Together, Go Chelsea!). Or you could remember that curly C goes with curly G and straight A with straight T.

Now try this

1 State where in an animal or plant cell you would find DNA.   **(1 mark)**

2 Describe the structure of a DNA molecule.   **(3 marks)**

There are three marks available so you need to give **three** different facts. Think about how many strands there are, how they are joined, and the shape that this produces.

Chromosomes and genes

CHROMOSOMES and GENES are made of DNA. Genes give the instructions to a cell to tell it what to do.

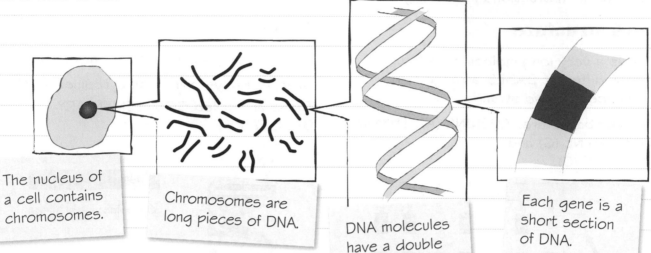

The nucleus of a cell contains chromosomes.

Chromosomes are long pieces of DNA.

DNA molecules have a double helix shape.

Each gene is a short section of DNA.

Genes

A gene is a short piece of DNA at a particular point on a chromosome. It codes for a particular characteristic such as eye colour.

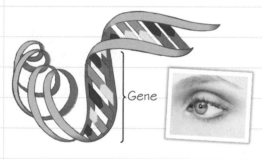

Gene

Chromosomes

Genes are found on chromosomes. One chromosome contains thousands of different genes.

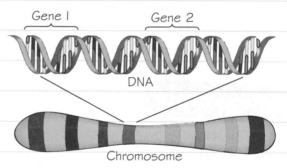

Gene 1   Gene 2

DNA

Chromosome

There are 23 pairs of chromosomes in all human cells, apart from in the sex cells (egg and sperm) which have 23 single chromosomes. Chromosomes come in pairs because you inherit one from each parent.

Worked example

Use the words in the box to complete the sentences below.   (3 marks)

| chromosomes | genes | nucleus |

DNA is found in the <u>nucleus</u> of a cell. Long strands of DNA make <u>chromosomes</u>. Chromosomes are made up of <u>genes</u>, which are the code for the characteristics of an organism.

Now try this

1 What is a gene?   (2 marks)   2 Explain the function of chromosomes.   (2 marks)

Alleles, genotypes and phenotypes

A PHENOTYPE is a characteristic that is visible and does not change, like eye colour. A person's phenotype is determined by their genes. Genes from parents are passed on to their offspring, which results in similarities in phenotype within families.

Alleles and genotypes

Chromosomes in all cells, except for the sex cells, come in pairs. This means the cell has two copies of every gene.

The alternative genes for each characteristic are called ALLELES. The combination of two alleles in a fertilised egg is called the GENOTYPE.

If the two chromosomes have the same alleles for a certain gene, the genotype is HOMOZYGOUS.

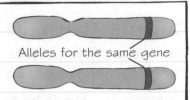
Alleles for the same gene

If the two chromosomes have different alleles for the gene, the genotype is HETEROZYGOUS.

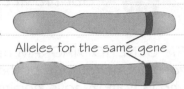
Alleles for the same gene

Dominant or recessive?

If the alleles are different, the DOMINANT allele 'trumps' the RECESSIVE allele.

So if the dominant allele is in the genotype this characteristic will be shown in the phenotype.

We write the genotype as a pair of letters for the pair of alleles. A dominant allele is given a capital letter and a recessive allele is given a lower-case letter.

Flower colour is controlled by a single gene. Let R represent the dominant allele for red petals and r the recessive allele for white petals. The table below shows possible genotypes and phenotypes for these alleles.

Genotype	Phenotype
RR	Red petals
Rr	Red petals
rr	White petals

Homo means same, hetero means different.

Now try this

1 Describe what homozygous means. **(2 marks)**

2 Describe what phenotype means. **(2 marks)**

Always give examples when you can. It shows that you understand the definition.

Punnett squares and pedigree diagrams

The offspring of a male and a female will receive one allele from each parent. The dominant allele in each pair will determine the phenotype of the offspring.

Genetic diagrams

Remember, both parents have two alleles for each gene, so there are four possible ways that these alleles can be paired in their offspring.

 Let B be the dominant allele for brown eye colour.

 Let b be the recessive allele for blue eye colour.

The GENETIC DIAGRAM opposite shows the possible genotypes of the offspring from one parent who is homozygous dominant and one parent who is homozygous recessive for eye colour. In this case, all offspring will have brown eyes.

> The dominant allele is shown with a capital letter and the recessive with a lower-case letter.

Parents	Mother	Father
Phenotype	Brown	Blue
Genotype	BB	bb
Gametes	B B	b b
Possible combinations		
Genotype	Bb Bb	Bb Bb
Phenotype	Brown Brown	Brown Brown

Pedigree diagrams

A PEDIGREE DIAGRAM shows the inheritance of a phenotype in a family. Cystic fibrosis is an inherited genetic disorder caused by a recessive allele.

The family tree opposite shows three generations. Sammy must have two copies of a recessive allele (homozygous). Neither of his parents has the disease, so they must both be CARRIERS (heterozygous).

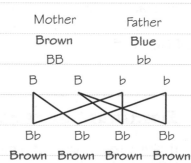

■ Male with cystic fibrosis
● Healthy female
■ Healthy male

Sammy

Worked example

> A Punnett square shows the same type of genetic information shown above, but in a table.

In mice, fur colour is controlled by one gene. The dominant allele (G) gives grey fur, the recessive allele (g) gives white fur.
Complete the Punnett square of the possible genotypes of the offspring from a male mouse with homozygous dominant alleles for fur colour and a female mouse with homozygous recessive alleles for fur colour. **(3 marks)**

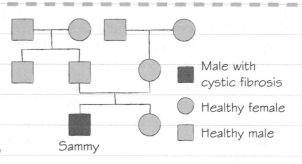

		Father genotype	
	Parent gametes	G	G
Mother genotype	g	Gg	Gg
	g	Gg	Gg

Now try this

1. From the information in the worked example above, draw a genetic diagram of the possible phenotypes and genotypes of the offspring from a male grey mouse with heterozygous alleles for fur colour and a female grey mouse with heterozygous alleles for fur colour. **(2 marks)**

2. Describe what a pedigree analysis diagram can be used to show in a family. **(1 mark)**

Predicting genetic outcomes

Based on the genotypes of parents, it is possible to predict the PROBABILITY of their offspring inheriting a particular allele.

Using Punnett squares

Cystic fibrosis is caused by a recessive allele (t). The Punnett square shows an example where both parents are heterozygous carriers of the disease.

The offspring have possible genotypes TT, Tt or tt in the RATIO 1 TT : 2 Tt : 1 tt. So there is a 1 in 4 (0.25) PROBABILITY that the offspring will have the disease (genotype tt).

		Parent genotype Tt	
Parent gametes		T	t
Parent genotype Tt	T	TT	Tt
	t	Tt	tt

You may be asked to analyse the outcomes of genetic crosses using probabilities, ratios or percentages.

In this example:
- probability is ¼ or 0.25
- ratio is 1 in 4
- percentage is 0.25 × 100 = 25%

Worked example

(a) If the allele for purple flowers is dominant to the allele for pink flowers, complete the Punnett square opposite to show the possible offspring from a cross between a heterozygous purple and a homozygous pink flowered plant. Use P for the dominant allele and p for the recessive allele. **(2 marks)**

(b) What is the probability of getting a plant with pink flowers? Explain your answer. **(2 marks)**

There are 2 in 4 possibilities of having pp (pink flowered plants).

So the probability of having pink flowers is

2/4 = 0.50

This is a 50% probability.

	Purple flowers	
	P	P
Pink flowers p	Pp	pp
p	Pp	pp

Now try this

1 Two alleles (D) and (d) code for a particular feature. The dominant allele is D and d is recessive for an inherited condition. If one parent is a carrier for this genetically inherited condition and one parent is not a carrier:

(a) Draw the Punnett square to show the possible genotypes of the offspring. **(2 marks)**

(b) Calculate the probability of the parents having a child with the condition. **(1 mark)**

(c) Calculate the probability of the parents having a child who is healthy. **(1 mark)**

Genetic mutations

A MUTATION occurs when the base sequence on a DNA molecule is changed.

Genes are sections of DNA and DNA is made up of bases arranged in sequences on two strands.

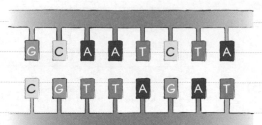

If part of the base sequence on a DNA molecule is removed or changed, this results in changes in the genetic code, which is called a mutation.

To illustrate how a change in the genetic code can have a significant effect on a gene, look at the sentence below:

> science includes biology, chemistry and physics.

If the s and the c are swapped over, the sentence now reads:

> csiense insludec biology, shemictry and phycisc.

This sentence no longer makes sense. The same principle applies with genetic mutations.

Effect of mutations

Some mutations result in a change in the physical characteristics of an organism. This can be beneficial or it can be harmful.

Harmful	Beneficial
👎 Sickle cell disease and cystic fibrosis are both caused by genetic mutations.	👍 Mutations might result in new characteristics that help an organism adapt to their environment.
👎 Some forms of cancer are caused by genetic mutations.	👍 The sickle cell trait gives protection against malaria.

Mutations can be beneficial. For example, the fur of the Arctic fox turns white in winter, as camouflage.

Now try this

1 Complete the table below with the complementary base pairs for a strand of DNA. **(1 mark)**

Base	A	T	C	G	C	C	A	T	A
Complementary base pair									

2 Describe how changes in the sequence of bases can result in genetic mutations. **(2 marks)**

Homeostasis

HOMEOSTASIS means keeping the same internal environment in the body. Your body needs to maintain its internal environment so that your cells can function properly.

Temperature

Salt levels

Things that need to stay the same in the body

Water content

Blood sugar levels

Feedback

If your body detects a change in its internal environment, it uses a FEEDBACK MECHANISM to correct the imbalance.

- RECEPTORS detect a change.
- PROCESSING CENTRES receive information and determine the correct response.
- EFFECTORS produce the response.

Levels too high → Receptor ← Levels too low

Receptor ⇩ Processing centre ⇩ Effector

Levels increase ← Effector → Levels decrease

Homeostasis systems

The NERVOUS system and ENDOCRINE system work together to maintain homeostasis. Communication between receptors and effectors can be via NERVE CELLS or HORMONES.

Hormones are secreted from GLANDS, which are part of the endocrine system. They travel in the blood and act on specific body parts to produce a response to bring the body back to a normal condition.

Worked example

Which **two** of the following statements about hormones is true? **(1 mark)**

☐ A Hormones travel along nerves.

☒ B Hormones are used to regulate cells and organs.

☐ C Hormones act equally on all cells and organs in the body.

☒ D Hormones are produced by glands.

Hormones are chemical messengers which travel in the blood, so A is not true.

Now try this

1 Explain the meaning of the term homeostasis. **(2 marks)**

You need to say what the word means and **why** it is important.

2 Write down **two** things that your body maintains using homeostasis. **(2 marks)**

The nervous system

The nervous system is made up of the CENTRAL NERVOUS SYSTEM (CNS) and the PERIPHERAL NERVOUS SYSTEM (PNS).

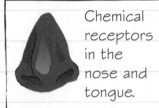

Don't confuse the spinal cord and the vertebrae. The spinal cord is protected by the vertebral column.

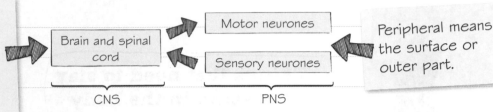

Brain and spinal cord

Motor neurones

Sensory neurones

Peripheral means the surface or outer part.

CNS   PNS

RECEPTORS are found in sense organs and detect a stimulus (a change in the environment).

 Chemical receptors in the nose and tongue.

Sound receptors in the ear.

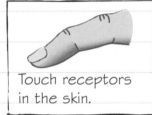 Touch receptors in the skin.

 Light receptors in the eyes.

Sensory neurones transmit electrical impulses to the CNS.

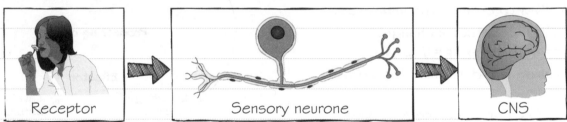

Receptor   Sensory neurone   CNS

An EFFECTOR is a muscle or gland. Effectors produce an action (movement) or secretion (hormone). Motor neurones transmit electrical impulses from the CNS to the effector.

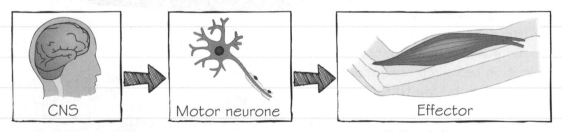

CNS   Motor neurone   Effector

Worked example

A motorcyclist suffers a road accident which results in a severe injury to their neck. Following the accident they have poor coordination in their legs. Explain why this happens, even though the nerves in the legs are not actually damaged. **(2 marks)**

If nerves in the spinal cord are damaged, this can prevent electrical impulses from the brain reaching the leg muscles, and can result in paralysis of the legs.

Now try this

1 (a) Describe the function of a receptor. **(2 marks)**
   (b) Give **two** examples of where receptors may be found. **(2 marks)**

 Make sure that you always use the correct scientific words like 'impulses' and 'paralysis'.

Involuntary and voluntary responses

Some of the body's actions require us to think about them before they can happen. Others occur without us even realising.

Voluntary responses

These require a person or animal to think about doing the action. The brain is involved in processing the response.

Lifting

Running

Eating/drinking

Writing

This is also called conscious control.

Involuntary responses

These are controlled without the person or animal thinking about it.

Breathing

Sneezing

Heart beating

Blinking

This is also called unconscious control.

Reflexes

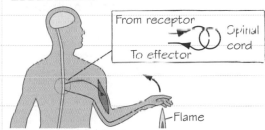

From receptor
To effector
Spinal cord
Flame

A REFLEX produces a rapid involuntary response to a stimulus and is usually there to protect us from harm, for example moving a body part away from a painful stimulus. This involuntary response is much faster than a voluntary response because it does not require any thought processing by the CNS.

Worked example

You need to know the sequence of components in a reflex arc **and** how a reflex response is different from a voluntary response.

Use the words in the box to complete the diagram below to describe a reflex arc.   **(5 marks)**

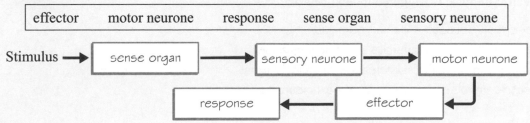

| effector | motor neurone | response | sense organ | sensory neurone |

Stimulus → sense organ → sensory neurone → motor neurone

response ← effector ←

Now try this

1 Which **one** of the following is a reflex action?   **(1 mark)**

A ☐ running away from a bee   B ☐ taking your hand away from a hot flame

C ☐ drinking water when you are thirsty   D ☐ putting on warm clothes when you are cold

2 Describe **two** differences between a voluntary and an involuntary response.   **(2 marks)**

Synapses

A neurone carries information by electrical impulses. The impulse is then transmitted to the next neurone by a chemical signal to trigger the electrical impulse along the next neurone.

However, there are small gaps between neurones called SYNAPSES. The electrical signal cannot pass directly from one neurone to another across this gap.

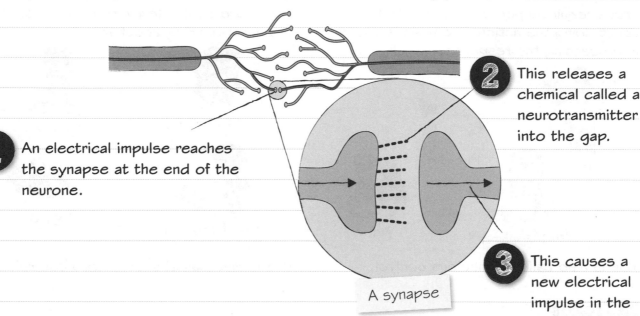

1 An electrical impulse reaches the synapse at the end of the neurone.

2 This releases a chemical called a neurotransmitter into the gap.

3 This causes a new electrical impulse in the next neurone.

A synapse

There are synapses in the brain and the spinal cord.

Worked example

Arrange the sentences below in the correct order to explain how a synapse is used in a reflex arc.

(3 marks)

1 Synapse in spinal cord releases chemical signal.
2 Receptor detects a painful stimulus.
3 Sensory neurone transmits electrical impulse.
4 Electric impulse is triggered in next neurone.

2 Receptor detects a painful stimulus.
3 Sensory neurone transmits electrical impulse.
1 Synapse in spinal cord releases chemical signal.
4 Electric impulse is triggered in next neurone.

Now try this

1 Explain how neurones transfer impulses across a synapse.

(3 marks)

Control of blood glucose

The concentration of glucose in the blood must be maintained. This is an example of HOMEOSTASIS. Remember, the ENDOCRINE SYSTEM helps to control homeostasis.

The endocrine system

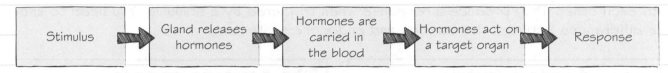

| Stimulus | ⮕ | Gland releases hormones | ⮕ | Hormones are carried in the blood | ⮕ | Hormones act on a target organ | ⮕ | Response |

The pancreas and blood glucose

The gland involved in blood glucose concentration is the PANCREAS and the hormones released are INSULIN and GLUCAGON, which target the liver.

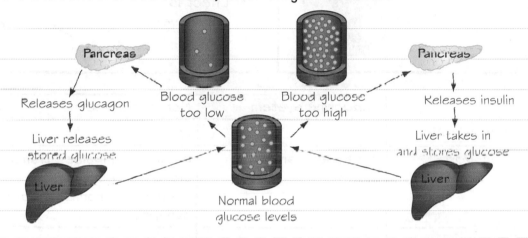

Pancreas — Releases glucagon — Liver releases stored glucose — Liver

Blood glucose too low

Blood glucose too high

Normal blood glucose levels

Pancreas — Releases insulin — Liver takes in and stores glucose — Liver

Remember: insulin ↓ lowers blood glucose concentration and glucagon ↑ raises it.

Worked example

(a) Identify how a person's blood glucose levels can increase. **(1 mark)**

After a person has eaten foods that contain carbohydrates.

(b) Describe the effect of the hormone insulin on the body. **(2 marks)**

If the blood glucose levels are too high, the pancreas releases insulin. Insulin targets the liver, which responds by storing the excess glucose and brings blood glucose levels back to normal.

(c) Describe the effect of the hormone glucagon on the body. **(2 marks)**

If the blood glucose levels are too low, the pancreas releases glucagon which targets the liver. The liver responds by releasing its stored glucose into the bloodstream bringing blood glucose levels back to normal.

Now try this

1   Which **one** of the following is the name of the gland where insulin is released? **(1 mark)**

   A ☐ liver   **B** ☐ red blood cell   **C** ☐ mouth   **D** ☐ pancreas

2   Identify how hormones travel to their target organ. **(1 mark)**

Differences between the endocrine and nervous systems

The nervous and endocrine systems both allow different parts of the body to communicate with each other. They produce a response when triggered by a stimulus. You need to know the differences between the nervous and endocrine systems.

The endocrine system

- Maintains homeostasis.
- Effect is long lasting.

The nervous system

- Allows the body to respond instantly to a change in the environment.
- Effect is short-lived.

	Endocrine system	Nervous system
Speed of communication	slow	rapid
Method of transport	hormones carried in blood	electrical impulses transmitted along neurones chemical transmission across synapses
Duration of response	minutes, hours or days	less than a second

Worked example

Describe how the nervous system allows the body to respond to a stimulus. **(4 marks)**

The nervous system sends impulses to the CNS via sensory neurones. The CNS responds by sending impulses to motor neurones to produce an effect. The signals are transmitted by electrical impulses along each neurone and travel across neurones by a chemical signal.

Make sure that you use scientific vocabulary – for example, use 'electrical impulses' not 'messages', and use 'neurones' not 'nerves'.

Now try this

1 Which **one** of the following phrases correctly gives the method of transmission in the nervous system? **(1 mark)**

A ☐ carried in the blood   B ☐ carried in the lymph

C ☐ electrical impulses along neurones   D ☐ hormones

2 Explain why the endocrine system produces slower responses in comparison to the nervous system. **(2 marks)**

Thermoregulation

You need to know how your body REGULATES its temperature. The chemical reactions in your body work best at 37°C, which is normal body temperature.

 ◄ Decrease in temperature   **37°C**   Increase in temperature ►

👎 HYPOTHERMIA
Body temperature
too low

👍 Normal body
temperature

👎 HYPERTHERMIA
Body temperature
too high

The body's response to cold

Here are three ways your body responds to regulate a FALL in temperature:

1 RAISING BODY HAIR – goosebumps help raise body hair which traps heat on the surface of the skin.

2 VASOCONSTRICTION – blood vessels narrow, taking blood away from the skin surface to reduce heat loss to the environment.

3 SHIVERING – muscle contraction causes an increase in body heat.

The body's response to heat

Here are three ways your body responds to regulate a RISE in temperature:

1 LOWERING BODY HAIR – this increases heat loss from the skin.

2 VASODILATION – blood vessels close to the skin surface widen so blood is brought closer to the skin surface and excess body heat is lost to the environment.

3 SWEATING – evaporation of sweat on the skin causes heat to be lost.

Worked example

Explain why a person's face can go red when they get hot.   **(2 marks)**

When you get hot, your blood vessels dilate. This means that blood is brought closer to the surface of the skin. This can make your skin appear red.

Detecting temperature change

Your body has two ways of telling if it is too hot or too cold:

☑ receptors in the skin detect changes in your skin temperature.

☑ receptors in your brain detect changes in your blood temperature.

Now try this

1 When this chef enters a walk-in freezer, her body temperature falls. Explain two ways her body responds to regulate this fall in temperature.   **(4 marks)**

The question asks you to **explain**. This means that you need to write down two different responses to the cold **and** describe how each process helps to increase body temperature.

Learning aim B: 6-mark questions 1

There will be an extended writing question on your exam paper. You can practise answering this question type over the next two pages.

To answer the question successfully you will need to:

✓ structure your answer in a logical and organised way

✓ write full sentences in your answer.

✓ use appropriate scientific terminology

Worked example

It is important for the body to maintain a constant internal environment so that the body cells are able to function properly.

In a healthy person, blood glucose concentrations are usually kept at between 4.4 and 6.1 mmol/l.

Explain how the endocrine system maintains blood glucose concentration. **(6 marks)**

This is an excellent answer.

The gland involved in blood glucose concentration is the pancreas. This gland releases hormones into the bloodstream which target the liver to control blood glucose levels.

When blood sugar levels are too high, the pancreas releases insulin which targets the liver. Insulin causes the liver to store the excess glucose and convert it to glycogen or fat. This returns the blood glucose levels to normal.

If blood glucose levels are too low, the pancreas releases glucagon, which is a hormone that targets the liver. The liver responds by releasing its stored glucose into the bloodstream. The release of stored glucose brings blood glucose levels back to normal.

Blood glucose levels would increase after eating a meal which contains carbohydrates or a sugary snack. This would result in insulin being released so that the liver stores the excess glucose. When a person exercises, blood glucose levels decrease because the glucose would be used for muscle contraction. This would result in the pancreas releasing glucagon. The release of glucagon causes the liver to release stored glucose into the blood stream and return blood glucose levels to normal.

Think about when and how blood glucose levels would increase or decrease.

This answer describes the gland, the target organ and the hormones involved in controlling blood glucose concentrations.

Correct scientific terminology has been used, including the correct names for the hormones involved in blood glucose control. Other key terms including 'target', 'store' and 'convert' are included which demonstrate a good knowledge of the processes involved in blood glucose control.

Rather than stating just 'eating a meal', this answer states that the meal has to contain carbohydrates. This demonstrates knowledge of what sorts of foods increase blood glucose levels.

It is important that the end result of the hormone release is stated so that it is clear that you know the function and purpose of this hormone.

Now try this

1   Explain how body temperature is maintained at 37 °C. **(6 marks)**

Learning aim B: 6-mark questions 2

Explain

Pay attention to the command word in the question - what are you being asked to do? If a question asks you to 'explain', you need to write down how the process works. To do this you will first of all have to describe the main components in the endocrine system, then explain how they are involved in maintaining blood glucose concentrations.

Drawing diagrams

It may help to draw a diagram to help to illustrate your answer. This will also help you to structure your answer as you can refer to the diagram in your answer.

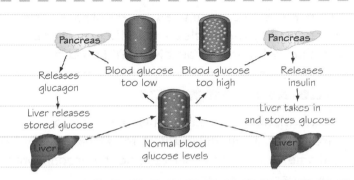

Here is another student's answer to the question on page 20.

This is a basic answer.

When the blood sugar levels go up then insulin goes out from the pancreas. When blood sugar levels go down glucogon goes out from the pancreas to make blood sugar levels go up.

The liver works with the pancreas to make this happen.

Blood glucose goes up if you eat some food and it goes down if you haven't eaten food for a while.

State what sort of foods need to be eaten in order for blood glucose levels to increase. This is important: some foods, such as those high in protein, will not actually affect blood glucose levels.

goes out

This is not a technical term – 'released' would be a better word to use. Always try to use technical terms where possible.

The key hormones and the ways in which they affect blood glucose concentrations included, which is good.

The terms 'blood glucose' and 'blood sugar' are both used in the same answer. Try to stick to just one of these terms so that it is clear that you know what you are talking about. The question refers to blood glucose, so it is better to use this term instead of blood sugar.

Now try this

1 Explain the difference in communication between the endocrine system and the nervous system.

(6 marks)

The structure of an atom 1

Everything is made up of ATOMS. Atoms are the building blocks of everything around us.

Sub-atomic particles

An atom is made up of a NUCLEUS and ELECTRONS. The nucleus in the middle of the atom is very small compared to the overall size of the atom. The nucleus contains PROTONS and NEUTRONS.

The nucleus is surrounded by electrons. They move around the nucleus in SHELLS. These shells are also referred to as ENERGY LEVELS.

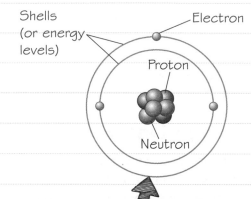

Shells (or energy levels) — Electron — Proton — Neutron

Atoms in elements

Each element contains only one type of atom. Iron is an element and it is made up of only iron atoms. A sample of the element carbon contains only carbon atoms.

Most of an atom is empty space, because the electron shells are a long way from the nucleus.

Worked example

What are the names of the particles that make up an atom? **(3 marks)**

There are three particles in an atom – neutrons, protons and electrons.

Worked example

List the following in order of increasing size:
atom
nucleus
proton **(1 mark)**

Proton, nucleus, atom.

The nucleus is very small compared to the size of an atom, and protons are found inside the nucleus.

Always read the question carefully. This question is asking you to give the number of each type of particle found in the **nucleus**.

Now try this

1 The diagram shows an atom. Fill in the table to show the type and number of particles in the atom. **(3 marks)**

Electrons	
Protons	
Neutrons	

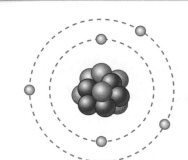

The structure of an atom 2

Atoms consist of neutrons, protons and electrons. The number of protons and electrons in an atom tells you what the CHARGE on the atom is.

Comparing neutrons, protons and electrons

	Location	Charge	Relative mass
Neutron	Nucleus	No charge (**neutral neutrons**)	1
Proton	Nucleus	Positive (**positive protons**)	1
Electrons	Outer shells	Negative	0.0005

You need to be able to compare the charges and masses of protons, neutrons and electrons. 'Relative to' means compared to. Protons and neutrons have the same mass, which is about 2000 times the mass of an electron.

Atoms of the same element

Atoms of a given element have the same number of protons in the nucleus and this number is unique to that element. For example, all sodium atoms have 11 protons, like the three below.

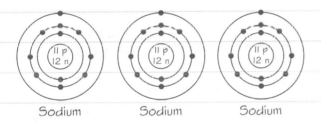

Sodium   Sodium   Sodium

The charge of an atom

There are always exactly the same number of protons and electrons in every atom. This means that the overall charge on an atom is 0 as the positive charge on the protons is balanced by the negative charge on the electrons.

For example, sodium has 11 protons and 11 electrons:

$$+ 11 + -11 = 0$$

Worked example

(a) If an atom has 14 electrons, how many protons does it have? **(1 mark)**

A ☐ 0   B ☐ 6   C ☐ 7   D ☒ 14

There are always the same number of protons as electrons in an atom.

(b) State the overall charge of an atom. Give a reason for your answer. **(2 marks)**

0. The number of protons with a positive charge always equals the number of electrons with a negative charge, so the positive and negative charges balance out.

Now try this

1 Which is the smallest part of an atom? **(1 mark)**

A ☐ proton   B ☐ electron

C ☐ neutron   D ☐ outer shell

2 Where are electrons found in an atom? **(2 marks)**

3 Which particle has no charge? **(1 mark)**

Atomic number and mass number

You need to know what the numbers on a chemical symbol mean.

Atomic number

Each element has a fixed number of protons in the nucleus.

This number is called the ATOMIC NUMBER.

As the number of protons equals the number of electrons, the atomic number is also the number of electrons in an atom.

Mass number ⟶ 7
Atomic number ⟶ 3 Li

Mass number

The number of particles in the nucleus of the atom is the mass number:

mass number = number of protons + number of neutrons

For example, as shown opposite, an atom of lithium (Li) has a mass number of 7.

Golden tip

The atomic number is ALWAYS smaller than the mass number.

Worked example

The diagram shows the symbol for an atom of calcium.

$$^{40}_{20}\text{Ca}$$

Calculate the number of protons and neutrons in an atom of calcium. **(2 marks)**

Number of protons = 20
Number of neutrons = 40 − 20 = 20

The atomic number is the number of protons, and this is the smaller of the two numbers given.

The mass number is the number at the top. Subtract the atomic number from the mass number to work out the number of neutrons.

Now try this

1. If an atom has an atomic number of 8, how many electrons does it have? **(1 mark)**

2. If an atom has an atomic number of 11 and a mass number of 23, how many neutrons does it have? **(1 mark)**

3. The diagram opposite shows the symbol for an atom of beryllium.
   How many of the following does an atom of beryllium have? $^{9}_{4}\text{Be}$ **(3 marks)**
   (a) protons
   (b) electrons
   (c) neutrons

The periodic table 1

The periodic table is a way of organising all of the elements. They are arranged according to their atomic number and their chemical properties. The elements are placed in order of increasing atomic number.

The periodic table

| | | | | | | | | | | | | | | | | | H | | | | | | | | | | | | | | | | | | | He |

Metals are on the left-hand side and in the centre.

Non-metals are on the right-hand side.

Now try this

1 The atomic number of silicon is 14. Use the periodic table to find the symbol for silicon. **(1 mark)**

The periodic table 2

The elements are arranged in the periodic table according to certain rules. You need to know why certain elements are in certain positions.

Periods

The rows of the periodic table are called PERIODS. Elements in a period have different chemical properties.

These are the elements in Period 4:

$^{39}_{19}$K Potassium	$^{40}_{20}$Ca Calcium	$^{45}_{21}$Sc Scandium	$^{48}_{22}$Ti Titanium	$^{51}_{23}$V Vanadium	$^{52}_{24}$Cr Chromium	$^{55}_{25}$Mn Manganese

The rows are called periods because periodic means having a repeating pattern.

Groups

Elements that have very similar chemical properties are placed in the same GROUP which is a vertical column in the periodic table.

These are the elements in Group 1.

$^{7}_{3}$Li Lithium
$^{23}_{11}$Na Sodium
$^{39}_{19}$K Potassium
$^{85}_{37}$Rb Rubidium
$^{133}_{55}$Cs Caesium
$^{223}_{87}$Fr Francium

Worked example

Use the periodic table on page 25 to name **three** elements in Group 2. **(3 marks)**

Beryllium, magnesium, calcium.

These are the first three elements in Group 2. You could have also named strontium, barium or radium.

Worked example

Which of the elements shown are both in the same group? **(1 mark)**

These letters are **not** the actual chemical symbols of the elements

A ☐ elements B and C   B ☐ elements W and X
C ☒ elements C and Z   D ☐ elements A and Y

Remember, vertical columns are groups and horizontal rows are periods.

Now try this

1 What is the name for the elements that are arranged in vertical columns in the periodic table? **(1 mark)**

A ☐ periods   B ☐ groups   C ☐ periodic table   D ☐ atoms

2 Use the periodic table on page 25 to state which of the following pairs of elements has similar chemical properties. **(1 mark)**

A ☐ sodium, Na and magnesium, Mg
B ☐ nitrogen, N and oxygen, O
C ☐ potassium, K and sodium, Na
D ☐ hydrogen, H and helium, He

You need to know that elements in the same group have similar chemical properties.

Isotopes and relative atomic mass

Some elements have the same atomic number but a different mass number. These are called ISOTOPES.

Isotopes

Isotopes of the same element have the same number of protons so they will be placed in the same position on the periodic table. They have different mass numbers because they have different numbers of neutrons.

These isotopes of carbon have the same number of protons (6) but different numbers of neutrons.

- An atom of carbon-12 has 6 neutrons (12-6). $\,^{12}_{6}C$
- An atom of carbon-13 has 7 neutrons (13-6). $\,^{13}_{6}C$

Worked example

Complete the table to show how many protons, electrons and neutrons contained in each of the isotopes of oxygen shown below. **(3 marks)**

$\,^{16}_{8}O$ $\,^{17}_{8}O$ $\,^{18}_{8}O$

   A   B   C

	Protons	Electrons	Neutrons
A	8	8	8
B	8	8	9
C	8	8	10

These oxygen isotopes have the same atomic number, so they all have the same number of protons and electrons. They have different numbers of neutrons because the mass numbers are different.

Relative atomic mass

The RELATIVE ATOMIC MASS of an element is the average mass of a large number of atoms of the element. As some elements have different isotopes, the amount of each isotope (PERCENTAGE ABUNDANCE) affects the overall or relative atomic mass.

$$\text{Relative atomic mass} = \frac{(\text{mass number of isotope I} \times \% \text{ abundance}) + (\text{mass number of isotope 2} \times \% \text{ abundance})}{100}$$

To calculate the relative atomic mass, you need to know the mass numbers of the isotopes present and their percentage abundances. If an element has no isotopes, the relative atomic mass is a whole number.

Worked example

MATHS SKILL

Use the data below to calculate the relative atomic mass of copper. **(2 marks)**

Isotope	$\,^{63}_{29}Cu$	$\,^{65}_{29}Cu$
Percentage abundance	70%	30%

$$\text{Relative atomic mass} = \frac{(63 \times 70) + (65 \times 30)}{100}$$
$$= \frac{6360}{100}$$
$$= 63.6$$

Now try this

1 Use the data below to work out the relative atomic mass of lithium. **(2 marks)**

Isotope	$\,^{6}_{3}Li$	$\,^{7}_{3}Li$
Percentage abundance	7.6%	92.4%

Filling electron shells 1

There is a limit to the number of electrons that can fill the shells around the nucleus. Make sure that you understand this and are confident filling electron shells.

The first shell

The first shell is next to the nucleus. This shell always fills first. There is room for just two electrons in this shell.

The second shell

When the first electron shell is full, electrons start to fill the second shell. This can hold up to eight electrons.

The third and fourth shell

When the second shell is full, electrons then fill the third shell. This can also hold eight electrons.

When the third shell is full, electrons enter the fourth shell.

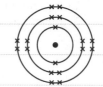

Worked example

Complete the diagram to show the electron shells with the correct number of electrons in each shell for an atom of sulfur (atomic number 16).

(2 marks)

The number of electrons is the same as the number of protons.

Now try this

1 How many electrons fill the first electron shell?   **(1 mark)**

   A ☐ 1   B ☐ 2   C ☐ 4   D ☐ 8

2 State how many electrons the second and third energy shells can hold.   **(2 marks)**

3 Complete the diagram to show the electron shells with the correct number of electrons in each shell for an atom of calcium (atomic number 20). Use × to represent an electron.   **(2 marks)**

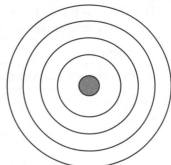

You need to know how to fill electron shells with up to 20 electrons.

Filling electron shells 2

Electronic configuration

There is a way of writing how electrons fill the shells around the nucleus without drawing a diagram. This is called the ELECTRONIC CONFIGURATION.

The electronic configuration for fluorine (atomic number 9) is 2.7.

Use the rules for filling electron shells to work out the electronic configuration.

This is the electronic configuration for calcium (atomic number 20):2.8.8.2.

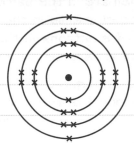

Golden tip

If you are told the atomic number of an element, you need to be able to work out the electronic configuration.

You need to know how to do this for up to 20 electrons. This electronic configuration is 2.8.8.2.

Worked example

Write the electronic configuration for the following atoms:

(a) helium (atomic number 2)

2

(b) nitrogen (atomic number 7)

2.5

(c) aluminium (atomic number 13)

2.8.3

(d) argon (atomic number 18)

2.8.8

(e) calcium (atomic number 20) **(5 marks)**

2.8.8.2

If you know the atomic number of an atom, you know the number of electrons of that atom.

1. The first shell is full after two electrons.

2. The second shell is full after eight electrons.

3. The second and third shells each hold up to eight electrons.

Now try this

1 Write out the electronic configuration of the following atoms:

  (a) hydrogen (atomic number 1)

  (b) magnesium (atomic number 12)

  (c) phosphorus (atomic number 15)

  (d) sulfur (atomic number 16)

  (4 marks)

Electron shells and groups

There is a connection between the number of outer electrons an element has and the position of that element in the periodic table.

Group number

Elements that have the same number of electrons in their outer shell are in the same group in the periodic table. Because elements in the same group have the same number of electrons in their outer shells, these elements all have very similar chemical properties.

The electronic configuration of the first three elements in Group 1 of the periodic table shows that these elements all have 1 electron in their outer shell.

Group 1 element	Electronic configuration
$^{7}_{3}\text{Li}$	2.1
$^{23}_{11}\text{Na}$	2.8.1
$^{39}_{19}\text{K}$	2.8.8.1

Worked example

Complete the table to show the atomic number and electronic structure of the first three elements in Group 2 in the periodic table.   **(6 marks)**

Group 2 element	Atomic number	Electronic configuration
$^{9}_{4}\text{Be}$	4	2.2
$^{24}_{12}\text{Mg}$	12	2.8.2
$^{40}_{20}\text{Ca}$	20	2.8.8.2

Remember: the atomic number (bottom number) is the number of protons, which is the same as the number of electrons.

You can check your answers to the electronic configuration by remembering that as this is Group 2, all these elements must have two electrons in the outer shell.

Now try this

1 The atomic symbol for aluminium is $^{27}_{13}\text{Al}$.
   (a) What is the electronic structure of this element?   **(1 mark)**
   (b) Which group is this element in?   **(1 mark)**

2 Use the periodic table to explain why potassium (left) and sodium (right) both react in a similar way with water.   **(2 marks)**

Potassium

Sodium

Metals and non-metals

Elements are classified as METALS or NON-METALS depending on their position in the periodic table.

Metals and non-metals in the periodic table

H																	He
Hydrogen																	Helium

☐ Metals
☐ Non-metals

Li	Be											B	C	N	O	F	Ne
Lithium	Beryllium											Boron	Carbon	Nitrogen	Oxygen	Fluorine	Neon
Na	Mg											Al	Si	P	S	Cl	Ar
Sodium	Magnesium											Aluminium	Silicon	Phosphorus	Sulfur	Chlorine	Argon
K	Ca	Sc	Ti	V	Cr	Mn	Fe	Co	Ni	Cu	Zn	Ga	Ge	As	Se	Br	Kr
Potassium	Calcium	Scandium	Titanium	Vanadium	Chromium	Manganese	Iron	Cobalt	Nickel	Copper	Zinc	Gallium	Germanium	Arsenic	Selenium	Bromine	Krypton
Rb	Sr	Y	Zr	Nb	Mo	Tc	Ru	Rh	Pd	Ag	Cd	In	Sn	Sb	Te	I	Xe
Rubidium	Strontium	Yttrium	Zirconium	Niobium	Molybdenum	Technetium	Ruthenium	Rhodium	Palladium	Silver	Cadmium	Indium	Tin	Antimony	Tellurium	Iodine	Xenon
Cs	Ba	La	Hf	Ta	W	Re	Os	Ir	Pt	Au	Hg	Tl	Pb	Bi	Po	At	Rn
Caesium	Barium	Lanthanum	Hafnium	Tantalum	Tungsten	Rhenium	Osmium	Iridium	Platinum	Gold	Mercury	Thallium	Lead	Bismuth	Polonium	Astatine	Radon

The metals and non-metals are separated by a zig-zag line starting from boron.

You can see that most of the elements in the periodic table are actually metals.

Copper is a metal. It has chemical symbol Cu.

Helium is a non-metal. It has chemical symbol He.

Worked example

Use the periodic table to classify the following elements as metals or non-metals.

(a) boron (B)   (1 mark)
non-metal

(b) carbon (C)   (1 mark)
non-metal

(c) rubidium (Rb)   (1 mark)
metal

The question tells you to use the periodic table. You are not expected to remember which elements are metals or non-metals.

Now try this

1 Name a group in the periodic table that contains only metals.   (1 mark)

2 Name a group in the periodic table that contains only non-metals.   (1 mark)

Compounds and formulae

Elements are shown on the periodic table as one or two letter symbols. This is a shorthand way of writing the elements' names. You need to be able to use the periodic table to find the element's name from its symbol, or find the symbol for a particular element. You also need to remember the formulae for a small number of simple compounds.

Symbols of elements

The names of some elements are easy to remember, as the symbol is the first letter(s) of their name.

Zn – zinc   O – oxygen
H – hydrogen   Cl – chlorine
N – nitrogen   Ca – calcium
C – carbon

Some elements have chemical symbols which do not always appear to make sense, but this is because the symbol comes from the Latin name for the element.

Cu – copper
K – potassium
Na – sodium

Compound formulae

The FORMULA of a compound tells you what elements it contains and how many atoms of each element are in the compound. When there is no number against an element's symbol, it means there is one atom of that type present.

For example, the compound sodium chloride, NaCl, has one sodium atom to each chlorine atom.

CO_2 is the formula for carbon dioxide. The subscript 2 shows that for each carbon atom there are two oxygen atoms.

A MOLECULAR ELEMENT is an element that usually exists as two or more atoms chemically bonded together to form a molecule.

Examples of molecular elements are:

$$H_2 \qquad O_2 \qquad N_2$$

The 2 in these formulae means that there are two atoms of that type joined together in the molecule.

Worked example

The formula for sulfuric acid is H_2SO_4. Complete the table to show the type and number of each atom in this compound.

(3 marks)

Atom	Number of atoms
Hydrogen, H	2
Sulfur, S	1
Oxygen, O	4

Compounds to remember

hydrochloric acid	HCl
sulfuric acid	H_2SO_4
nitric acid	HNO_3
sodium carbonate	Na_2CO_3
copper (II) carbonate	$CuCO_3$
calcium carbonate	$CaCO_3$
hydrogen	H_2
carbon dioxide	CO_2
copper (II) oxide	CuO
zinc oxide	ZnO
sodium hydroxide	$NaOH$

Now try this

1 State the type and number of each atom in a compound with the formula $CuCO_3$.   **(3 marks)**

2 Which of the following is an example of a molecular element?   **(1 mark)**

   A ☐ CO_2 B ☐ O_2 C ☐ NaCl   D ☐ H_2O

A molecular element is made up of the same atoms.

Elements, compounds and mixtures

Elements

An ELEMENT is made up of only one type of atom. There are 92 elements in the periodic table.

Elements

(H) hydrogen   (He) helium   C carbon   O oxygen

Each element is unique and has its own chemical and physical properties. Remember: elements with similar properties are placed in the same group of the periodic table.

Compounds

A COMPOUND is formed by two or more elements that have reacted and joined together. The elements are bound together by chemical bonds.

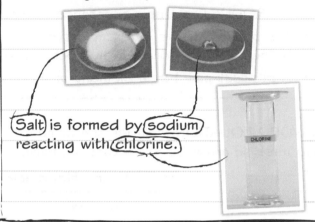

Salt is formed by sodium reacting with chlorine.

Mixtures

A MIXTURE is made when two or more elements or compounds are combined together but are not joined together by chemical bonds. This means the chemical properties of the elements or compounds do not change in a mixture.

If sand and water are mixed together, they can be easily separated back into sand and water

Molecules

A MOLECULE is made up of two or more atoms joined together by chemical bonds. The atoms may be the same, such as in a hydrogen molecule.

hydrogen molecule

Or the atoms may be different such as one carbon atom and two oxygen atoms joined together to make a molecule of carbon dioxide.

O C O

Carbon dioxide molecule

Worked example

Describe the difference between a mixture and a compound.   **(2 marks)**

A mixture is where two substances are mixed together but are not joined by chemical bonds. A compound is where two or more atoms react and are joined together by chemical bonds.

Where substances are added together but are not joined by chemical bonds it is called a mixture.

Now try this

1 Explain the differences between an element and a compound.   **(2 marks)**

2 Oil and water added together is an example of: **(1 mark)**

A ☐ a compound

B ☐ a mixture

C ☐ a molecule

D ☐ an element

Word equations

A CHEMICAL REACTION results in atoms becoming rearranged to form new substances. Word equations are used to show this change in the arrangement of the atoms and the new substances that have been made.

Key terms

- The REACTANTS are the substances that take part in a reaction.
- A PRODUCT is a new substance formed by a chemical reaction.
- The products have different properties compared to the reactants. In the reaction below, zinc is a solid and hydrochloric acid is a liquid, but one of the products is a gas.
- A product may be an element or a compound.

A WORD EQUATION includes the names of the reactants and the products, and uses an arrow to show that a chemical reaction has taken place.

$$\underbrace{\text{zinc + hydrochloric acid}}_{\text{REACTANTS}} \rightarrow \underbrace{\text{hydrogen + zinc chloride}}_{\text{PRODUCTS}}$$

In a compound name, the metallic element is named first and the non-metallic element is named second.

The same types of atoms that are in the reactants will be in the products. You cannot make atoms of different elements out of these reactants.

zinc + hydrochloric acid → hydrogen + zinc chloride

magnesium + hydrochloric acid → hydrogen + magnesium chloride

sodium hydroxide + hydrochloric acid → sodium chloride + water

sodium hydroxide + hydrofluoric acid → sodium fluoride + water

Worked example

Give the word equation to show what happens when iron filings and hydrochloric acid react together. **(1 mark)**

iron + hydrochloric acid → iron chloride + hydrogen

Iron and hydrochloric acid are the reactants, so they go on the left-hand side of the equation.

The arrow goes from the reactants to the product.

Iron chloride and hydrogen are the products of this reaction.

Now try this

1 Give the word equation to show what happens when iron filings and sulfuric acid react together. **(1 mark)**

You need to know that the compounds produced from the reaction of metals with sulfuric acid are called SULFATES, and the compounds produced from the reaction of metals with hydrochloric acid are called CHLORIDES.

Balanced chemical equations

A BALANCED CHEMICAL EQUATION shows the numbers and types of atoms involved in a chemical reaction. You need to be able to write balanced chemical equations for certain types of reaction you have covered in this topic.

sodium hydroxide + hydrochloric acid → sodium chloride + water

$$NaOH + HCl → NaCl + H_2O$$

You can see by counting the symbols for each hydrogen atom (H) that two hydrogen atoms are in the formulae for the reactants and they have combined in the product, which is water.

> In a chemical reaction, the atoms involved are not created nor destroyed, so the numbers of atoms of the same type have to be the same on both sides of the equation.

Balancing an equation

To balance a chemical equation, you should add up the number of atoms on each side of the equation to make sure they are the same.

If they are not you insert a number at the front of the formula of the reactants and products where needed.

For example in the reaction of magnesium with oxygen, try writing:

Mg + O₂   MgO
1 Mg atom → 1 Mg atom
2 O atoms   1 O atom

This equation is not balanced because there is not the same number of atoms of each element on each side of the equation. You need to add in numbers to make the equation balance:

2 Mg + O₂   2 MgO
2 Mg atoms → 2 Mg atoms
2 O atoms   2 O atoms

> To make sure the equation balances, check you have the correct numbers of each element on each side of the equation.

Golden tip

When balancing chemical equations, change only the numbers at the front of the chemical symbols. **Never** change the small numbers (the subscripts) in a chemical equation as this would change the actual formula of the substance.

For example:
To make two lots of H_2O by changing it to H_4O_2 makes this a very different substance! Instead, write $2H_2O$. This formula still has four hydrogen and two oxygen atoms but is still water.

Worked example

MATHS SKILL

The formula for magnesium chloride is $MgCl_2$. Give the balanced equation for the reaction between magnesium and hydrochloric acid. **(3 marks)**

$$Mg + 2HCl → MgCl_2 + H_2$$

Now try this

1 The formula for zinc chloride is $ZnCl_2$. Give the balanced equation for the reaction:

zinc + hydrochloric acid → hydrogen + zinc chloride **(3 marks)**

2 When copper (II) oxide reacts with sulfuric acid, copper sulfate ($CuSO_4$), is formed. Give the balanced equation for the reaction. **(3 marks)**

Acids, bases and alkalis

All substances can be put into one of three categories: acid, base or neutral. Some bases dissolve in water to form an alkali. An INDICATOR can be used to show if a substance is acidic, alkaline or neutral.

The pH scale

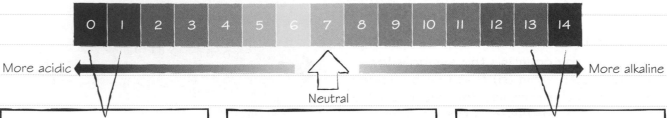

More acidic ←――――――――――――――――――――――――――→ More alkaline

Neutral

Acids

- ✓ ACIDS have a pH of less than 7.
- ✓ Stronger acids have a lower pH.
- ✓ Strong acids turns universal indicator red and weaker acids turn it orange or yellow.
- ✓ An acid turns blue litmus paper red:

  acidic

Neutral

- ✓ Neutral solutions have a pH of 7.
- ✓ Neither acidic nor alkaline.
- ✓ Turn universal indicator green.
- ✓ Does not change the colour of litmus paper:

  neutral

Alkalis

- ✓ An ALKALI has a pH of more than 7.
- ✓ Stronger alkalis have a higher pH.
- ✓ Strong alkalis turn universal indicator purple, weaker alkalis turn it blue-green.
- ✓ An alkali turns red litmus paper blue:

  alkaline

Bases

A BASE is a substance that can react with an acid to neutralise it. Most bases, like copper oxide, will not dissolve in water.

An alkali is a subset of bases. It has all the properties of a base except that an alkali will dissolve in water.

Bases	Soluble in water
Copper oxide	No
Sodium hydroxide	Yes
Zinc hydroxide	No

Sodium hydroxide is a base **and** an alkali because it dissolves in water.

Worked example

Describe **two** differences between an acid and an alkali. **(2 marks)**

An acid has a pH of between 1 and 6 and turns universal indicator red, orange or yellow. An alkali has a pH of between 8 and 14 and turns universal indicator bluey green, dark blue or purple.

Now try this

1 What colour will blue litmus paper turn if it is dipped into an acidic solution? **(1 mark)**

   A ☐ red   **B** ☐ blue   **C** ☐ purple   **D** ☐ green

2 A solution turns universal indicator green.
   (a) State whether the solution is acidic, alkaline or neutral. **(1 mark)**
   (b) The pH of stomach acid is 1. Give the colour of universal indicator in stomach acid and state what this value tells you about the strength of this acid. **(2 marks)**

Neutralisation reactions

A neutral solution has a pH of 7 and is neither acidic or alkali. It is possible to NEUTRALISE an acid or base by carrying out a NEUTRALISATION REACTION.

When you add an acid to a base they may react to produce a neutral substance. This is called a neutralisation reaction. If you keep adding acid, however, there is no more base to react and you end up with too much acid.

👎 too much acid or too little base → no neutralisation

👍 correct amount of acid and correct amount of base → neutralisation

👎 too little acid or too much base → no neutralisation

Products of neutralisation reactions

A neutralisation reaction usually produces a SALT and water. A salt is the chemical name given to a compound produced when a base reacts with an acid.

$$acid + base \rightarrow salt + water$$

The type of salt that is produced depends upon which acid and which base are used in the reaction.

(nitric acid) + (sodium hydroxide) → (sodium nitrate) + water

acid   base   salt

Watch out – sodium chloride (the salt you put on your chips) is not the only substance that scientists call a salt.

Worked example

Describe why it is important to have exactly the right quantities of acid and base in a neutralisation reaction. **(2 marks)**

If not enough base is added to an acid the product will remain slightly acidic.

If not enough acid is added to a base the product will remain slightly alkaline.

Now try this

1   When a base reacts with an acid in a neutralisation reaction, which **one** of the following is produced?   **(1 mark)**

   A ☐ a salt

   B ☐ a base

   C ☐ an acid

   D ☐ an alkali

2   Identify the products of a neutralisation reaction.   **(2 marks)**

3   In the following reaction, identify the base.   **(1 mark)**

     sodium hydroxide + hydrochloric acid → sodium chloride + water

Equations for neutralisation reactions

The general word equation for a neutralisation reaction is:

base + acid → salt + water

Learn this pattern so that you can write word equations for reactions and predict the products. In neutralisation reactions, the first part of the name of the salt produced comes from the metal in the base and the second part comes from the name of the acid.

Changing the acid

- Hydrochloric acid produces chloride salts.
- Nitric acid produces nitrate salts.
- Sulfuric acid produces sulfate salts.

copper oxide + hydrochloric acid → copper chloride + water

copper oxide + nitric acid → copper nitrate + water

copper oxide + sulfuric acid → copper sulfate + water

The name of the salt is made up of the name of the base (copper) and the name of the acid (sulfuric → sulfate).

Remember that the products of a neutralisation reaction are always a salt and water.

Changing the base

- Copper oxide and zinc oxide are metal oxides and these are both bases.
- Sodium hydroxide is a metal hydroxide and is a soluble base.
- When these are added to an acid, they produce a salt and water.

metal oxide + acid → salt + water
metal hydroxide + acid → salt + water

copper oxide + hydrochloric acid → copper chloride + water

zinc oxide + hydrochloric acid → zinc chloride + water

sodium hydroxide + hydrochloric acid → sodium chloride + water

Worked example

Write out the word equations for the following neutralisation reactions.

(a) sodium hydroxide and hydrochloric acid. **(1 mark)**

sodium hydroxide + hydrochloric acid → sodium chloride + water

(b) copper oxide and sulfuric acid. **(1 mark)**

copper oxide + sulfuric acid → copper sulfate + water

(c) zinc oxide and nitric acid. **(1 mark)**

zinc oxide + nitric acid → zinc nitrate + water

Now try this

1 What is the name of the salt formed when copper oxide and hydrochloric acid are used in a neutralisation reaction? **(1 mark)**

   A ☐ copper sulfate   B ☐ hydrochloric sulfate

   C ☐ copper chloride   D ☐ copper acid

An alkali is a subset of bases, which are soluble in water.

2 Write the word equation for the reaction between sodium hydroxide and sulfuric acid. **(1 mark)**

Reactions of acids with metals

When an acid reacts with a metal, hydrogen gas and a salt are produced:

metal + acid → salt + hydrogen

The name of the salt is a combination of the name of the metal element followed by part of the name of the acid.

magnesium + hydrochloric acid →
magnesium chloride + hydrogen

iron + sulfuric acid →
iron sulfate + hydrogen

zinc + hydrochloric acid →
zinc chloride + hydrogen

In any reaction of a metal with an acid, hydrogen gas is produced as well as a salt. This is zinc reacting with sulfuric acid.

Reactivity

- Some metals will produce a vigorous reaction with acid (lots of gas produced very quickly).
- Some metals react very slowly with acids.
- Some metals, such as gold, silver and copper, do not react at all with acids.

The speed of the reaction depends on the REACTIVITY SERIES of metals – that is, how reactive the metal is.

	Metal	Reactivity
Most reactive	Calcium	Reacts violently with acids
↓	Magnesium Aluminium Zinc Iron Tin Lead	React, but the reaction becomes less violent as you go down the series
Least reactive	Copper Silver Gold Platinum	Do not react with acids

Worked example

Give the word equation for the reaction between zinc and sulfuric acid. **(1 mark)**

zinc + sulfuric acid → zinc sulfate + hydrogen

Hydrochloric acid always produces chloride salts. Sulfuric acid always produces sulfate salts.

Now try this

1   What is the name of the salt formed when zinc and hydrochloric acid react together? **(1 mark)**

2   Complete the table below to show the name of the salt produced by different reactions between metals and acids. If there is no reaction, write 'No reaction'. **(3 marks)**

Name of metal	Name of acid		
	hydrochloric acid	nitric acid	sulfuric acid
aluminium			
copper			
magnesium			

Reactions of acids with carbonates

You need to learn the reactions of three acids (hydrochloric acid, nitric acid and sulfuric acid) with three carbonates (sodium carbonate, copper carbonate and calcium carbonate). These reactions all follow the same pattern:

acid + metal carbonate → salt + carbon dioxide + water

Products formed

Metal carbonates react with acids to form three products:

- a salt
- carbon dioxide
- water.

Some neutralisation reactions just produce a salt and water, but this reaction also produces carbon dioxide gas.

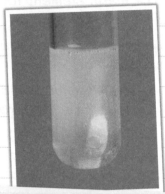

Calcium carbonate reacting in hydrochloric acid. The fizzing shows that a gas is produced.

Here are two reactions of an acid with a carbonate:

sulfuric acid + sodium carbonate → sodium sulfate + water + carbon dioxide

hydrochloric acid + calcium carbonate → calcium chloride + water + carbon dioxide

Worked example

Write the word equation for the reaction between nitric acid and calcium carbonate.   **(2 marks)**

nitric acid + calcium carbonate → calcium nitrate + water + carbon dioxide

Now try this

1   State the general word equation for a reaction of an acid with a carbonate.   **(2 marks)**

2   Write the word equation for the reaction between sulfuric acid and copper (II) carbonate.   **(2 marks)**

3   Complete the table to show the name of the salt produced by different reactions between metal carbonates and acids.   **(3 marks)**

Name of metal	Name of acid		
	hydrochloric acid	nitric acid	sulfuric acid
calcium carbonate			
copper carbonate			
sodium carbonate			

Tests for hydrogen and carbon dioxide

Reactions of acids with metals produce hydrogen gas, and reactions of acids with a carbonate produce carbon dioxide. In order to determine if one of these reactions has occurred, it is possible to carry out tests to see if hydrogen or carbon dioxide has been produced.

Test for hydrogen

To test for hydrogen, place a lighted wooden splint into the mouth of a test tube that contains the gas. If hydrogen is present, there will be a popping sound. This is because the flame from the wooden splint lights the hydrogen which makes it burn explosively, making the popping noise.

Test for carbon dioxide

To test for carbon dioxide, bubble the gas produced in a reaction through LIMEWATER.

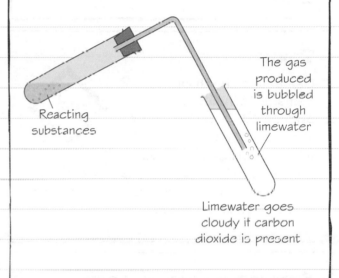

The gas produced is bubbled through limewater

Reacting substances

Limewater goes cloudy if carbon dioxide is present

Worked example

Describe which test you would carry out to determine which gas has been produced when an acid reacts with a metal. **(3 marks)**

Collect the gas produced from the reaction in a test tube then place a lit wooden splint into the mouth of this test tube. If the splint glows brightly and makes a popping noise then this confirms that the gas produced is hydrogen.

You should describe the test, the expected result, and what this means.

Now try this

1 **(a)** Name the solution that is used to test if carbon dioxide gas is produced in a reaction. **(1 mark)**

(b) Describe what you would observe if carbon dioxide was present. **(1 mark)**

Don't just write 'fizzing' – you would see this if any gas was produced. You need to say what observation would identify carbon dioxide as the gas that is produced.

Hazard symbols

Many substances can be harmful, so these are given symbols that are recognised all over the world. This is so that people from different countries who speak different languages will be able to recognise the hazard symbols and know to be careful when handling these substances.

Corrosive

Avoid contact with the skin as it attacks and destroys living tissue.

Strong acids and strong bases are both corrosive.

Flammable

These substances catch fire easily and should be stored in flame-resistant cupboards.

Magnesium is flammable.
Hydrogen gas is flammable.

Toxic

Can cause death or damage to health if swallowed, breathed in or absorbed by skin.

It's very unlikely that you will be permitted to do experiments with toxic substances, but you may see them in the chemical stores.

Moderate hazard

This substance is not corrosive but is harmful if inhaled or will cause irritation to the skin, eyes or inside the body.

Dilute acids and dilute sodium hydroxide are irritants.

Copper oxide is harmful.

Environmental hazard

These substances could cause immediate or delayed harm to ecosystems.

Copper oxide is hazardous to the environment.

In your practical work as well as for the exam, you need to be able to recognise the hazard symbols on this page.

Now try this

1 State what the symbol below means.   **(1 mark)**

2 Match the symbols A, B, C, D with the meanings numbered 1–4.   **(4 marks)**

A	B	C	D
....	....	....	....

1 Toxic   **2** Flammable   **3** Corrosive   **4** Environmental hazard

Applications of neutralisation reactions

Acids and bases occur naturally in everyday substances. Occasionally, a substance can be too acidic or too alkaline, and in these cases neutralisation reactions can be used to adjust the acidity or alkalinity of the substance.

Neutralisation reactions

Neutralisation of acidic soil

Some plants grow well in acidic soil but many do not. Farmers add a base, such as LIME (calcium oxide) or powdered CHALK (calcium carbonate), to acidic soil, which helps to reduce the acidity.

Indigestion remedies

Your stomach produces hydrochloric acid to help digest your food. If too much hydrochloric acid is produced, this can cause indigestion.

Indigestion is usually treated by taking antacids, as these can help to neutralise the excess acid.

Many antacids contain the bases magnesium hydroxide and magnesium carbonate.

Neutralising acidic waters

Gases that are produced from burning fuels can mix with clouds and produce ACID RAIN.

Acid rain falls into streams and lakes and can result in the water becoming acidic.

This acidic water can harm the organisms that live in the water.

Lime can be added to water to make the water less acidic.

Worked example

A bee sting contains an acidic substance. Describe how you could relieve the painful symptoms of the sting.

(2 marks)

As the sting is acidic, adding an alkaline substance will neutralise the sting.

> A neutralisation reaction requires an acid to be added to a base or a base to be added to an acid.

Now try this

1   Describe the effect on soil pH of adding lime to soil that is too acidic.   **(2 marks)**

2   Explain why some people take antacids to treat indigestion.   **(2 marks)**

Learning aim D: 6-mark questions 1

There will be an extended writing question on your exam paper. You can practise answering this question type over the next two pages.

To answer the question successfully you will need to:

☑ structure your answer in a logical and organised way

☑ write full sentences in your answer.

☑ use appropriate scientific terminology

Worked example

Acids and bases are used in science laboratories. We also use them in everyday substances: people suffer from acid indigestion or areas of land, such as a farmer's field, can become too acidic.

Explain how neutralisation reactions can be carried out to adjust acidity in different situations. **(6 marks)**

This is a very good answer.

A neutralisation reaction requires an acid to be added to a base or a base to be added to an acid.

A neutralisation reaction always produces a SALT and water. A salt is the chemical name given to a compound produced when a base reacts with an acid.

Acid + Base ⟶ Salt + Water

The stomach produces hydrochloric acid to digest foods. If too much hydrochloric acid is produced a person may suffer from acid indigestion. Antacids usually contain magnesium hydroxide, which is a base, so taking an antacid neutralises the acid and stops the acid indigestion.

Acid rain can form from the pollution of burning fossil fuels. This rain then falls on to the soil and makes the soil acidic. and while some crops grow well in acidic soil, many do not. Farmers use a base, such as LIME or powdered CHALK, to add to acidic soil which helps to reduce the acidity and makes the soil better for growing crops.

This acid rain can also fall into ponds and lakes which makes the water more acidic. Many fish and other organisms that live in the water cannot survive in acidic water, so lime is added to the water to neutralise the acid and make the water more suitable for the organisms to live in it.

You have been asked about neutralisation reactions so it is a good idea to show you know what a neutralisation reaction is in the first part of your answer. State what is required in a neutralisation reaction and write out the word equation of the reaction.

This answer has gone on to describe the applications of neutralisation reactions by using the information given in the question.

For each application the answer includes:
- why there is too much acid
- the problems associated with too much acid
- what is used in the neutralisation reaction
- the results of the neutralisation reaction.

Now try this

1 The periodic tables contains all of the elements ordered into groups and periods.

Explain why the elements in Group 2 are all in the same group in the periodic table? **(6 marks)**

44

Learning aim D: 6-mark questions 2

Explain

The key command verb in this question is 'explain'. This means that you need to describe the different neutralisation reactions and then include an explanation of how the neutralisation reactions work and why they are used.

This is another student's answer to the question on page 44.

This is a very basic answer.

A neutralisation stops an acid from being acidic so it is good if there is too much acid around.

You have to be careful in a science laboratory if you are using acids and bases as they are corrosive and can burn your skin so make sure you wear gloves and goggles if you are using them to keep you safe.

If you eat too much food, like a curry, you can get bad indigestion so you should take some Gaviscon or a Rennie which will make you feel better and stop the indigestion.

Farmers spray their fields with white lime powder to stop it being so acidic which is good for helping their crops grow.

The answer starts by attempting to describe a neutralisation reaction but uses incorrect terminology. A neutralisation reaction neutralises the acid rather than 'stopping it being acidic'. Always use scientific terms where possible.

Don't just write down everything you know about acids – make sure you stay focused on what the question has asked.

There is an attempt to explain the acid indigestion but the answer does not state why there is too much acid. Always state the scientific facts about antacids rather than naming brands of antacid.

Make sure that you **explain**. This answer attempts to explain the neutralisation reaction but there is no explanation of why the soil becomes acidic in the first place, why this is not good for the crops and then how the lime powder acts as a base to neutralise the acid.

Now try this

1   Gary is carrying out two chemistry experiments. In experiment A he mixes hydrochloric acid with sodium carbonate. In experiment B he mixes nitric acid with copper carbonate.

Explain what Gary will need to do in order to test the gas produced in each experiment.   **(6 marks)**

Balanced equations for reactions with acids

It is important that you know the formulae for all of the substances used in the reactions in learning aim D so that you are able to identify the substance from its formula and also write a balanced chemical equation for the reaction.

Acids

Hydrochloric acid	HCl
Nitric acid	HNO_3
Sulfuric acid	H_2SO_4

Metal oxides

Copper oxide	CuO
Zinc oxide	ZnO
Sodium hydroxide	NaOH

Products of reactions with acids

acid + base → salt + water

The formula of water is H_2O

acid + carbonate →
salt + water + carbon dioxide

The formula of carbon dioxide is CO_2

acid + metal → salt + hydrogen

The formula of hydrogen is H_2

Carbonates

Sodium carbonate	Na_2CO_3
Copper carbonate	$CuCO_3$
Calcium carbonate	$CaCO_3$

Remember: some elements occur as molecular elements. The formula for hydrogen gas is H_2 not H.

Worked example

The formula for sodium chloride is NaCl. Write the balanced equation for the reaction of hydrochloric acid with sodium carbonate. **(1 mark)**

$2HCl + Na_2CO_3 \rightarrow 2NaCl + H_2O + CO_2$

The answer cannot be

$HCl + Na_2CO_3 \rightarrow NaCl + H_2O + CO_2$

because if you count the numbers of sodium atoms (Na), or the number of hydrogen atoms (H), there are not the same number of atoms of each element on each side of the equation.

Worked example

The formula for sodium sulfate is Na_2SO_4. Write the balanced equation for the reaction of sulfuric acid with sodium carbonate. **(1 mark)**

$2H_2SO_4 + Na_2CO_3 \rightarrow$
$Na_2SO_4 + H_2O + CO_2$

You need to know the formula for the acids, bases and carbonates used in this unit, but you will always be given the formula of the salt product.

Now try this

1 Write the balanced equations for the following reactions.
    (a) hydrochloric acid and calcium carbonate   **(1 mark)**
    (b) zinc oxide and nitric acid   **(1 mark)**
    (c) sodium hydroxide and sulfuric acid   **(1 mark)**

To balance the equation, you may need to add some numbers into the equation. Always put the number at the **front** of the chemical formula, and never change the subscript numbers as this changes the chemical.

Forms of energy

Energy exists in many different forms.

1 THERMAL ENERGY is linked with hot or warm objects such as a fire, the Sun or hot water.

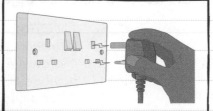

2 ELECTRICAL ENERGY is generated from a battery, solar cell or power plant.

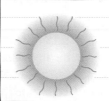

3 LIGHT ENERGY comes from a hot object like the Sun or light bulbs, or can be emitted by LEDs and lasers.

4 Energy is transformed into SOUND ENERGY when an object or substance vibrates, such as a drum or the vocal chords.

Forms of energy

5 KINETIC ENERGY is a form of MECHANICAL ENERGY, and is associated with the movement of an object.

6 POTENTIAL ENERGY is also a form of MECHANICAL ENERGY and is associated with the position of an object (vertical height) or how it is stretched or squashed.

7 NUCLEAR ENERGY is released when a nucleus is split (nuclear fission) or two nuclei fuse together (nuclear fusion).

Now try this

1 Which of the following is an example of thermal energy?
(1 mark)

A ☐ a ringing bell   **B** ☐ a burning coal fire
C ☐ a battery   **D** ☐ a stretched elastic band

2 Name the forms of energy that reach us from the Sun. **(2 marks)**

Light energy and solar energy are not always the same!

Solar energy only comes from sunlight and includes light energy and thermal energy.

Light energy can come from the Sun, but could also be from an artificial light source.

Uses of energy

Each form of energy has many different uses. Energy can be TRANSFORMED (changed) into other forms, and also TRANSFERRED to a different object.

 THERMAL ENERGY is used to heat buildings, cook food, and can be used to generate electricity.

 ELECTRICAL ENERGY is used for many different appliances in the home such as microwave ovens and light bulbs. These devices transform electrical energy into different forms of energy such as thermal energy and light energy.

 LIGHT ENERGY is used to see things. Light energy from the Sun can also be used to generate electricity (solar power), and is used by plants to make food (photosynthesis).

 SOUND ENERGY is used to communicate information.

 MECHANICAL ENERGY is used to move a force through a distance, such as in cars or the motor in a washing machine. The kinetic energy of moving steam, wind or water can also be used to generate electricity.

NUCLEAR ENERGY can be used as a weapon, or to generate electricity.

Energy transformations

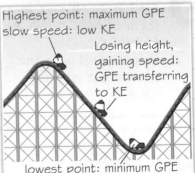

Highest point: maximum GPE slow speed: low KE

Losing height, gaining speed: GPE transferring to KE

lowest point: minimum GPE highest speed: maximum KE

In a rollercoaster ride, GRAVITATIONAL POTENTIAL ENERGY (GPE) is transformed into kinetic energy as the carriage speeds up. The wheels and track get hot, showing that some of the GPE is also transformed into thermal energy. You can show this as a diagram.

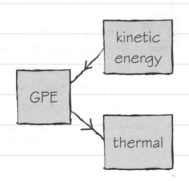

GPE → kinetic energy
GPE → thermal

Worked example

Complete the flow chart below to show the energy transformations when an electric kettle is used. **(2 marks)**

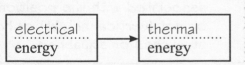

| electrical energy | → | thermal energy |

Now try this

1 Identify **two** ways in which thermal energy is used in the home. **(2 marks)**

2 The four devices listed opposite all transfer electrical energy to a different form. Draw lines to match each device with the main form of energy transferred. **(4 marks)**

oven	kinetic energy
food mixer	light energy
computer	thermal energy
MP3 player	sound energy

Energy stores

Energy can be stored and then used when it is needed. There are only a few stores of energy: chemical, gravitational potential, kinetic, thermal, elastic potential and nuclear. Electricity is not a store of energy. Electricity has to be generated using other energy forms. Light and sound energy also cannot be stored.

CHEMICAL ENERGY is stored in food and fuels. A chemical reaction releases the stored energy.

Batteries and fuel cells also store chemical energy, which can be transferred into electrical energy.

GRAVITATIONAL POTENTIAL ENERGY is energy that is stored in an object because of its position.

Water held behind a dam has stored gravitational potential energy that is transformed into kinetic energy when the water is released. In turbines, this kinetic energy is used to generate electricity.

A stretched or a squashed spring has stored **ELASTIC POTENTIAL ENERGY.**

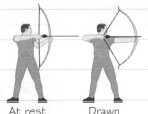

At rest   Drawn

A drawn bow also stores elastic potential energy that can be transferred to kinetic energy of the arrow.

If there was no air resistance, the arrow would keep moving and would be a store of kinetic energy – until the arrow hit something.

The **NUCLEAR ENERGY** stored in an atom is released in nuclear reactions. The thermal energy produced can be transferred to water in a boiler and the steam used to drive turbines.

If hot water is kept insulated, it is a store of thermal energy.

Worked example

Describe the energy transformations when a firework is lit. **(4 marks)**

Stored chemical energy is transformed into sound energy, light energy, kinetic energy and thermal energy.

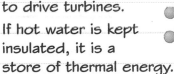

Do not just list four forms of energy produced. The question asks you to describe the **transformation**, so you need to describe the starting point as well as the end points.

Now try this

1   Describe the energy transformations when a rocket is launched. **(3 marks)**

2   Give **three** stores of chemical energy. **(3 marks)**

3   Give **two** stores of elastic potential energy. **(2 marks)**

4   Describe the energy transformations when a child bounces on a trampoline. **(3 marks)**

Thermal energy transfers

Energy can be TRANSFERRED from one place to another by processes such as heating, pushing or lifting. Thermal energy is transferred.

A difference in thermal energy between an object and its surroundings causes an energy transfer.

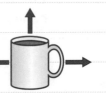
A hot object in a colder environment gives out thermal energy and cools down

A cold object in a hot environment takes in thermal energy and warms up

---

1 CONDUCTION transfers thermal energy when objects at different temperatures are in contact with one another.

A pan conducts heat from the hotplate to the food inside the pan.

In conduction, thermal energy is transferred when the atoms of a solid substance vibrate but the solid itself does not move.

Particles closest to the heat source vibrate as they heat up.

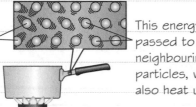

This energy is passed to neighbouring particles, which also heat up.

---

2 CONVECTION transfers thermal energy in a liquid or gas such as water or air. This sets up a CONVECTION CURRENT, which is movement of the hot and cooler parts of the fluid.

Warm air rises and spreads out

It loses some of its thermal energy to the rest of the air

Air near a radiator gets warmer and less dense

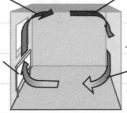

The cooler air is denser, so it sinks

---

3 RADIATION transfers thermal energy through the air or even through a vacuum.
Infrared radiation transfers thermal energy without any atoms moving. The energy is carried through a vacuum by a WAVE.

Infrared radiation is part of the electromagnetic spectrum (see page 62) and travels at the speed of light.

Worked example

Explain, in terms of the particles in a solid, how energy transfer takes place in conduction.
(2 marks)

Particles in the hotter part of the solid vibrate more and pass on their extra energy to their neighbours, which also heat up.

Now try this

1 Name the process by which energy is transferred by the Sun to the Earth.
(1 mark)

2 Explain, in terms of the particles in a liquid, how energy transfer takes place in convection.
(2 marks)

Measuring energy

In the process of energy transfer, energy is never created or destroyed. The unit for measuring energy transfer is JOULES (J).

The principle of conservation of energy

Energy can be transferred but it can never be created or destroyed. So, the total amount of energy before an energy transfer is always the same as the total amount of energy afterwards:

total energy in = total energy out

Energy transfer diagrams

A Sankey diagram or energy transfer diagram shows the amount of energy – in joules – before and after an energy transfer. The thicker the arrow, the greater the amount of energy involved.

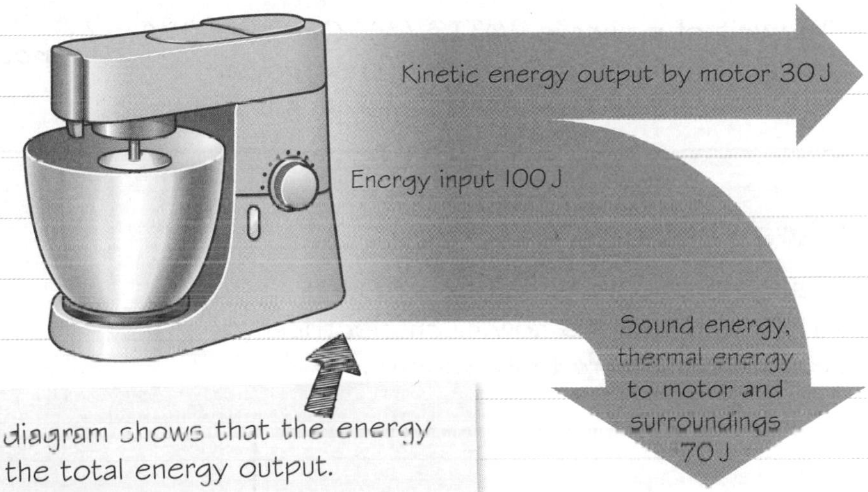

Kinetic energy output by motor 30 J

Energy input 100 J

Sound energy, thermal energy to motor and surroundings 70 J

This energy transfer diagram shows that the energy input is the same as the total energy output.

Worked example

MATHS SKILL

A car transfers 100 000 J of chemical energy from burning petrol. 37 000 J are transferred to the car as kinetic energy, and 1500 J are transferred to the lights and radio. Calculate how much energy in other forms is transferred to the car and the surroundings. **(3 marks)**

Energy input   = 100 000 J

Energy output = 100 000 J

So amount of other forms of energy transferred to the car and the surroundings

= 100 000 J – 37 000 J – 1500 J

= 61 500 J

Now try this

1 Which **one** of the following is the unit for measuring energy? **(1 mark)**

   A ☐ joules

   B ☐ watts

   C ☐ kg

   D ☐ minutes

2 State the principle of conservation of energy. **(1 mark)**

Power

Power is the measure of the amount of energy transferred per unit of time.

A person walking upstairs moves the same force (their weight) over the same distance if they run or walk. This requires the same amount of mechanical energy. However, if a person runs up the stairs the POWER generated is greater than if they had walked up the stairs because the mechanical energy is transferred in a shorter time.

Measuring power

The unit of power is WATTS (W). One watt (1W) equals 1 joule (J) per second (s) so power is a measure of how quickly energy is transferred.

$$\text{power (watts)} = \frac{\text{energy (joules)}}{\text{time (seconds)}}$$

Power ratings

All electrical appliances have a POWER RATING which shows how much electrical energy is transferred per second.

Golden tip

Remember: 1 kilowatt (kW) = 1000W

40W or 0.04kW

2000W or 2kW

Worked example

 MATHS SKILL

A motor transfers 50 J of electrical energy in 5 seconds. Calculate its power and give the units. **(3 marks)**

$$\text{power (watts)} = \frac{\text{energy (joules)}}{\text{time (seconds)}}$$

$$= \frac{50\,J}{5\,s}$$

Power = 10W

You need to know this equation and be able to use it. Take care that you use the correct units for each quantity.

Be careful – if the time is given in minutes, you must convert it to seconds by multiplying by 60.

Now try this

1 A hairdryer transfers 9000 J of electrical energy in 3 minutes. Calculate its power and give the units. **(3 marks)**

2 State how the power of a machine can be calculated. **(2 marks)**

Paying for electricity

Electricity companies calculate the electrical energy used in KILOWATT-HOURS (kWh).

Kilowatt-hours

1 kWh is the amount of energy transferred by a 1 kW appliance that is used for 1 hour. This is also called one UNIT of electricity.

energy transferred (kWh) = power (kW) × time (h)

number of units of electricity (kWh) = power (kW) × time (h)

> Kilowatts are a unit of power. Kilowatt-hours are a unit of energy.

The cost of electricity can be worked out by first finding out the energy transferred in kWh and then multiplying this by the cost of electricity per unit.

BTECLec   ELECTRICITY BILL

Previous reading	Current reading	Units used	Cost per unit	Total cost
45100	45500	400	7 pence	£28.00

Worked example

It takes 2 minutes to boil a 3 kW kettle and electricity costs 18p per unit. Calculate the cost of the energy used to boil this kettle. **(3 marks)**

2 minutes = 2/60
        = 0.03 hours
cost = 3 kW × 0.03 × 18p kWh
     = 1.62p

The cost of electricity is given per kilowatt-hour, so you will need to convert 2 minutes into hours and use this number in your calculation.

Worked example

Calculate the cost of the energy used by a 2 kW TV left on for 1 hour if one unit of electricity costs 20p. **(3 marks)**

energy transferred = power × time
                   = 2 × 1
                   = 2 kWh
cost of electricity = number of kWh × cost per unit
                    = 2 × 20p
                    = 40p

Now try this

1 Calculate the cost of the electricity used by the following appliances if the cost per unit is 10p:
  (a) 1 kW computer that is left on for 1 hour   **(2 marks)**
  (b) 5 kW heater that is left on for 2 hours   **(2 marks)**
  (c) 100 W bulb that is left on for half an hour   **(2 marks)**

Remember that 100 W is 0.1 kW

To calculate the number of kilowatt-hours, a time in minutes must be converted to a time in hours.

Efficiency of energy transfers

When energy is transferred or transformed, some energy is always wasted. The more efficient the transfer or transformation of energy, the less energy is wasted.

USEFUL ENERGY is energy that is transferred to the place we want and in the form we want it.

If the efficiency of a light bulb was 100% all the electrical energy transferred would be transformed into light energy.

This never happens!

WASTED ENERGY is energy that is transferred to a place where it is not intended or into a form that is not intended.

When electrical energy is transferred to a light bulb, some of the energy is transformed to thermal energy, which is wasted energy.

Calculating efficiency

The EFFICIENCY of a machine is defined as the proportion of energy transferred as useful energy. The efficiency can be calculated by the following equation:

$$\text{efficiency} = \frac{\text{useful energy} \times 100\%}{\text{total energy supplied}}$$

Electrical appliances such as fridges and freezers are given energy efficiency ratings. The higher the rating, the greater the efficiency, as more of the input energy is converted to useful energy.

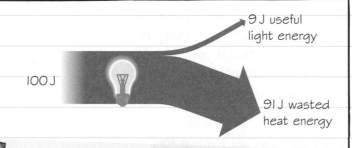

100 J → 9 J useful light energy / 91 J wasted heat energy

Efficiency does not have any units – it is measured as a percentage, which is a ratio.

Worked example

MATHS SKILL

The diagram shows the energy transfers in a television.

200 J of electrical energy → 100 J of heat energy } wasted energy / 40 J of sound energy, 60 J of light energy } useful energy

Calculate the efficiency of this television. **(3 marks)**

100 J is useful energy

Total energy supplied is 200 J

Therefore, efficiency = $\dfrac{100\,\text{J} \times 100\%}{200\,\text{J}}$

= 50%

No machine can be more than 100% efficient, so if your answer is more than 100% then your calculation is not right!

Now try this

1 Calculate the efficiency of the following two light bulbs, which both have an input of 80 J of electrical energy. **(4 marks)**
   (a) Light bulb A transfers 20 J to heat energy and 60 J to light energy.
   (b) Light bulb B transfers 50 J to heat energy and 30 J to light energy.

2 Use the data in this diagram to compare the efficiency of these two light bulbs. **(4 marks)**

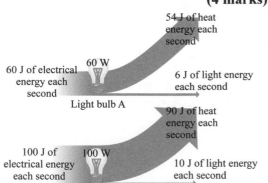

60 J of electrical energy each second → 60 W → 54 J of heat energy each second / 6 J of light energy each second
Light bulb A

100 J of electrical energy each second → 100 W → 90 J of heat energy each second / 10 J of light energy each second
Light bulb B

Renewable energy resources

There are two main types of energy resource: renewable and non-renewable. Both types of resources can be used to generate electrical energy. Renewable energy resources are resources that will not run out because they are always being replaced.

1 SOLAR cells transform light energy directly into electrical energy.

2 WIND turbines transform kinetic energy of the wind directly into electrical energy.

3 BIOFUELS made from plant material or animal waste can be used as a fuel for heating or processed into oil or gas.

4 HYDROELECTRIC power stations transform kinetic energy of falling water directly into electrical energy.

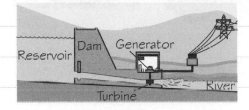

5 WAVE power transforms kinetic energy of the waves directly into electrical energy.

6 TIDAL power transforms kinetic energy of tidal currents or the rise and fall of the tide directly into electrical energy.

7 GEOTHERMAL energy is thermal energy from heated rocks in volcanic areas which is transferred to thermal energy of steam. This drives turbines to generate electrical energy.

(a) Tidal barrage (or tidal dam)
Estuary — High tide — Turbine ← Water — Sea

(b) Water stored at high tide — Low tide — Water → — Sea

Storing energy

Electrical energy cannot be stored by solar panels or the turbines used in power stations. This is why other sources of electrical energy are needed as back up – for example, at night. Batteries or fuel cells are stores of chemical energy.

Worked example

This is a solar-powered car. Describe how electrical energy generated by the solar cells can be stored so that the car can be used at night.

(2 marks)

Some of the electrical energy generated when the Sun is shining is used to recharge the batteries. The stored energy in the batteries can be used to power the car at night.

Now try this

1 Wind turbines are powered by a renewable energy resource.
   (a) Name **two** other renewable energy resources. **(2 marks)**
   (b) Explain how electricity can be generated by a wind turbine. **(2 marks)**

Non-renewable energy resources

These types of energy resources will run out one day. However, most of the energy that we use today is generated by non-renewable energy resources.

The chemical or nuclear energy in non-renewable energy resources can be transformed to thermal energy, which boils water to make steam. This steam drives turbines to generate electricity.

Fossil fuels (coal, gas and oil)

Nuclear fuels (uranium or plutonium)

Disadvantages

👎 Non-renewable energy resources are resources that will eventually run out because they cannot be replaced. Fossil fuels take millions of years to be formed, so it is not possible to make any more of these fuels for another million or more years.

👎 Burning fossil fuels produces carbon dioxide gas, which is a greenhouse gas, and sulfur dioxide gas, which causes acid rain.

👎 Nuclear power stations do not produce any polluting gases, but they do produce radioactive waste which will remain harmful to humans and animals for millions of years. This has to be stored safely to prevent leaks to the environment.

👎 Removing radioactive materials also makes nuclear power stations expensive to close down.

Worked example

Give **two** reasons why people should try and use more renewable energy resources compared to non-renewable energy resources. **(2 marks)**

Non-renewable energy resources will run out one day, so it is necessary to increase use of renewable energy resources to make fossil fuels last longer and so that energy can be generated when the non-renewable energy resources have been used up.

Now try this

1 Which **one** of the following is a non-renewable energy resource? **(1 mark)**

   A ☐ solar energy
   B ☐ tidal energy
   C ☐ nuclear energy
   D ☐ biofuel

2 Identify **two** types of fossil fuel. **(2 marks)**

Like fossil fuel, biofuels come from plant materials. However, biofuels such as wood or bioethanol can be renewed simply by growing more plants.

Using energy effectively

Non-renewable energy resources will run out one day and renewable energy resources do not yet generate sufficient electricity to meet demand. It is important to reduce overall energy use and to reduce use of fossil fuel resources to make supplies last longer.

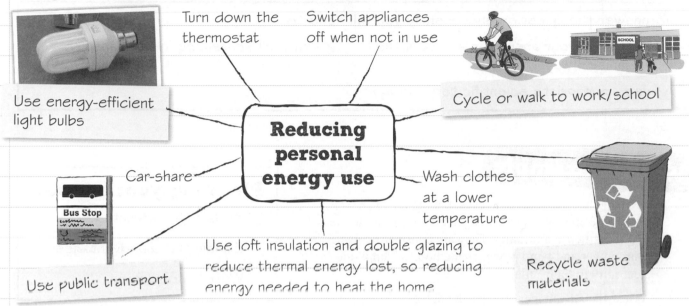

Use energy-efficient light bulbs

Turn down the thermostat

Switch appliances off when not in use

Cycle or walk to work/school

Car-share

Reducing personal energy use

Wash clothes at a lower temperature

Use public transport

Use loft insulation and double glazing to reduce thermal energy lost, so reducing energy needed to heat the home

Recycle waste materials

Fossil fuel inefficiency

Coal, gas and oil power stations are not very efficient. Over half of the input energy is wasted.

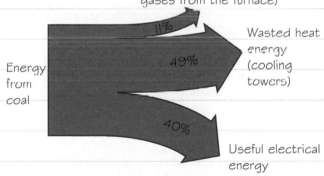

Wasted heat energy (hot gases from the furnace)

11%

Energy from coal

49%

Wasted heat energy (cooling towers)

40%

Useful electrical energy

Petrol and diesel engines in cars are also not very efficient, as all of the heat in the hot exhaust gases is wasted energy.

Fuel cells

When hydrogen and oxygen react in a fuel cell, an electrical current is produced.

Some vehicles now use hydrogen fuel cells. The hydrogen in a fuel cell can be made from water, which will never run out. However, to extract the hydrogen takes energy – a lot of it. Energy is also needed to compress the hydrogen gas for storage. This energy will probably come from fossil fuels.

Worked example

Explain why fossil fuel power stations are not very efficient. **(2 marks)**

Not all the energy stored in the coal is used to generate electricity. A lot of energy is wasted as heat in smoke from burning the coal, and in the cooling towers.

Now try this

1 Identify **three** ways in which it is possible to reduce use of electrical energy in the home. **(3 marks)**

2 Other than to reduce costs, explain why it is important for businesses and homes to reduce their use of electrical energy. **(2 marks)**

Learning aim E: 6-mark questions 1

There will be an extended writing question on your exam paper. You can practise answering this question type over the next two pages.

To answer the question successfully you will need to:

- ☑ structure your answer in a logical and organised way
- ☑ use appropriate scientific terminology
- ☑ write full sentences in your answer.

Worked example

A village has decided to invest some money in renewable energy resources to supply electricity to the homes in their community. They are considering using solar power and wind power as methods of supplying electricity to their village.

Assess the advantages and disadvantages of solar power and wind power to supply all the electricity to a home.

Planning your answer

- ☑ Explain the advantages.
- ☑ Explain the disadvantages.
- ☑ Write a conclusion.

This is a basic answer.

Solar power only gives energy in the daytime or when the sun is out.

Wind power only gives out energy when there is wind.

This means that energy will not be given out to the houses when it is not sunny or windy so there will be times when a house won't get any electricity.

gives out

This terminology is incorrect. Wind turbines do not 'give out' energy - they generate electricity. Make sure you get your terminology correct.

This answer has given the disadvantages of each energy resource but has not covered any advantages. The question asks for advantages as well so this needs to be included in the answer.

This answer does not evaluate the positive or negative aspects of these methods of energy production. It is mainly a description of the disadvantages of these types of energy resource and not an assessment of the situation.

Now try this

1 Energy transformations are never 100% efficient.
   Explain the processes of energy transformation and efficiency in a car engine. **(6 marks)**

Learning aim E: 6-mark questions 2

The key command verbs in this question are:

- assess   • advantages   • disadvantages

☑ ASSESS means that some form of evaluation needs to take place. You will need to pull out the important information given in the question. You will need to explain the things asked for in the question and then complete your answer with an overall conclusion.

☑ ADVANTAGES are the positive things associated with the two methods suggested in the question.

☑ DISADVANTAGES are the problems associated with the two methods suggested in the question.

Here is another student's answer to the question on page 58.

This is a very good answer.

The advantage of using renewable energy resources is their sustainability. Currently, non-renewable energy resources provide most of the energy that is used in the UK. However, as these resources will run out one day, it is necessary to start using renewable energy resources so that energy can be produced when non-renewable energy resources have been used up. All non-renewable energy resources also produce some form of pollution through burning fossil fuels or the waste products from nuclear power stations. Solar power and wind power are renewable methods of energy production which do not cause any pollution to the environment. In addition, they will not run out, so they are a good choice for this village.

Solar power will only generate energy during the daytime when there is sunlight, so this method of generating electricity will not work during the night or on very cloudy days which is a disadvantage of this energy source.

Wind power will only generate electricity when it is windy, but it will work 24 hours a day. Therefore, if the village just had one of these methods of generating electricity there would be 'downtime' when no electricity was generated. With solar power, this would happen at night when there is no sunlight, which would be a problem for people who use a number of electrical appliances during this period. It would therefore be a good idea to have an alternative energy supply as well as solar and wind power to generate electricity when there is no wind or sunlight. This will ensure that homes receive a constant electricity supply.

This answer clearly starts with the advantages of the renewable energy resources by stating the problems associated with non-renewable energy resources including pollution and the fact that they will run out one day.

Appropriate scientific terminology has been used throughout – for example, the sources of energy 'generate electricity' which is technically correct.

The disadvantages of each renewable energy resource are clearly stated.

An overall assessment and conclusion is provided at the end with a reasoned argument to justify the suggestion.

Now try this

1   Archers use a bow and arrow to shoot arrows into a target. In some competitions the target is quite a distance from the archer so it is important that the archer is able to transfer enough energy to the arrow in order for it to reach the target.

Explain the energy transfers involved when an archer shoots an arrow at a target.   **(6 marks)**

Wave characteristics

Waves transfer energy from one place to another.

1 Amplitude

Amplitude gives a measure of how much energy the wave carries.

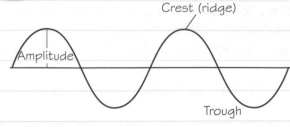

Crest (ridge)

Amplitude

Trough

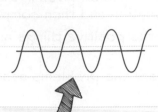

Low amplitude wave   High amplitude wave

The AMPLITUDE of a wave is the height of the wave at its maximum distance from its rest position. Amplitude is measured in metres.

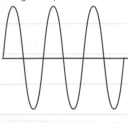

Watch out – amplitude is **not** the distance between the top and bottom of a wave. This is **twice** the amplitude.

2 Frequency

As waves are continually moving, the number of waves that pass a set point in one second is used to assess the FREQUENCY of a wave. Frequency is measured in HERTZ (Hz). One hertz (1Hz) = 1 wave per second.

1kHz = 1000 waves per second
1MHz = 1000000 waves per second
1GHz = 1000000000 waves per second

3 Wavelength

WAVELENGTH is the distance from the peak of one wave to the peak of the next wave. This is the same as the distance from trough to trough. Wavelength is measured in metres.

Crest   Wavelength   Crest

Trough

Worked example

The diagram below shows two waves, A and B, over the same time period.

A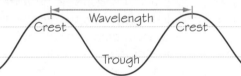

B

Which wave has the longest wavelength? **(1 mark)**
Which wave has the greatest frequency? **(1 mark)**

Wave A has the longest wavelength.
Wave B has the greatest frequency.

The higher the frequency **the more waves there are per second**, so there is less distance between the peaks of each wave. This means that waves with a high frequency have a short wavelength.

Now try this

1 Label the diagram of a wave with the following:
   (a) amplitude   **(1 mark)**
   (b) wavelength   **(1 mark)**
   (c) crest   **(1 mark)**

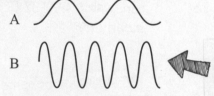

2 State the units for each of the following quantities:
   (a) wavelength   **(1 mark)**   **(b)** wave speed   **(1 mark)**
   (c) frequency   **(1 mark)**   **(d)** amplitude   **(1 mark)**

Wave calculations

You need to be able to carry out calculations using the wave speed, frequency and wavelength.

WAVE SPEED is the distance travelled by a crest or trough in one second. It is measured in metres per second, (m/s).

The WAVE EQUATION links speed to the frequency of the wave and the wavelength.

wave speed = frequency × wavelength
   (m/s)   (Hz)   (m)

> Make sure you can rearrange the wave equation.

Re-arranging the wave equation

If you have two of the numbers in the wave speed equation, you can re-arrange the equation to work out the missing value.

1 wave speed = frequency × wavelength

2 $\text{wavelength} = \dfrac{\text{wave speed}}{\text{frequency}}$

3 $\text{frequency} = \dfrac{\text{wave speed}}{\text{wavelength}}$

Golden tip

If the wave speed remains the same, increasing the frequency of a wave decreases the wavelength.

short wavelength – high frequency   long wavelength – low frequency

Worked example

MATHS SKILL

Calculate which of the following waves has the fastest wave speed. Show your working.   **(4 marks)**
A   A wave with a frequency of 10 Hz and a wavelength of 10 cm
B   A wave with a frequency of 20 Hz and a wavelength of 20 cm

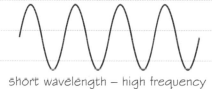

wave speed = frequency × wavelength
   Wave A = 10 × 0.10
           = 1 m/s
   Wave B = 20 × 0.20
           = 4 m/s
Wave B has the fastest wave speed.

> Make sure you use the correct units in the equation. To get the wave speed in metres per second, you must convert the wavelength in centimetres to metres: 10 cm = 0.1 m.

Now try this

1   Calculate the speed of a wave with frequency 100 Hz and wavelength 10 m.   **(3 marks)**

2   Calculate the frequency of a wave with a speed of 100 m/s and a wavelength of 5 m, and give its units.   **(4 marks)**

> Show your workings for any calculations that you carry out, so if you make any mathematical mistakes you may still gain marks for your workings.

> You are given two out of the three values from the wave speed equation so you need to rearrange the equation to work out the frequency of the wave.

The electromagnetic spectrum

The ELECTROMAGNETIC SPECTRUM is a range of electromagnetic waves with continuous wavelengths and frequencies. Each range of waves has different uses as well as different harmful effects which depend on their wavelength and frequency.

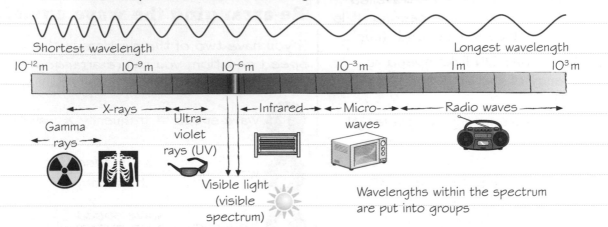

Shortest wavelength   Longest wavelength

10^{-12} m 10^{-9} m 10^{-6} m 10^{-3} m   1 m 10^{3} m

Gamma rays   X-rays   Ultra-violet rays (UV)   Visible light (visible spectrum)   Infrared   Micro-waves   Radio waves

Wavelengths within the spectrum are put into groups

Another way of ordering the electromagnetic spectrum is from the lowest frequency and longest wavelength to the highest frequency and shortest wavelength.

Approximate frequency in Hz

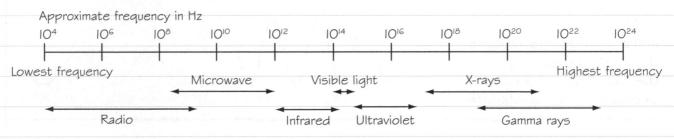

10^{4} 10^{6} 10^{8} 10^{10} 10^{12} 10^{14} 10^{16} 10^{18} 10^{20} 10^{22} 10^{24}

Lowest frequency   Highest frequency

Radio   Microwave   Infrared   Visible light   Ultraviolet   X-rays   Gamma rays

To remember the order of the spectrum, use a mnemonic such as:

Red	Martians	Invade	Venus	Using	X-ray	Guns
Radio waves	Microwaves	Infrared	Visible	Ultraviolet	X-rays	Gamma rays

Worked example

MATHS SKILL

Electromagnetic waves travel at the speed of light, 3×10^8 m/s.

Calculate the frequency of an electromagnetic wave with a wavelength of 10 cm. Use standard form for your answer. **(3 marks)**

wave speed (m/s) = frequency (Hz) × wavelength (m)

so, frequency (Hz) = $\dfrac{\text{wave speed (m/s)}}{\text{wavelength (m)}}$

$= \dfrac{300\,000\,000}{0.1}$

$= 3\,000\,000\,000$

This is 3×10^9 Hz

Now try this

1   Which waves have the lowest frequency in the electromagnetic spectrum?   **(1 mark)**

A ☐ gamma rays

B ☐ radio waves

C ☐ microwaves

D ☐ X-rays

2   Which waves have the highest frequency in the electromagnetic spectrum? **(1 mark)**

A ☐ radio waves

B ☐ X-rays

C ☐ gamma rays

D ☐ microwaves

Radio waves

RADIO WAVES are a form of electromagnetic radiation. Radio waves are mainly used for different methods of communication by transmitting information 'wirelessly' through the air.

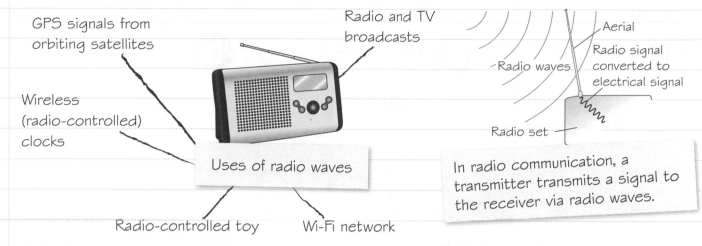

GPS signals from orbiting satellites

Radio and TV broadcasts

Aerial

Radio signal converted to electrical signal

Radio waves

Wireless (radio-controlled) clocks

Uses of radio waves

Radio set

In radio communication, a transmitter transmits a signal to the receiver via radio waves.

Radio-controlled toy   Wi-Fi network

Characteristics

Radio waves have:

- the lowest frequency in the electromagnetic spectrum
- the longest wavelengths (which can be as long as 100 km!).

Dangers of radio waves

The higher the frequency of the wave, the more energy the wave transfers. The more energy that can be transferred, the more harm the wave can do to human health.

Radio waves have no proven harmful effects as they have very low frequencies, and so very low energy.

Worked example

MATHS SKILL

Electromagnetic waves travel at the speed of light, 3×10^8 m/s.

Calculate the wavelength of radio waves from a radio station that broadcasts on a frequency of 107.6 MHz. **(3 marks)**

wave speed (m/s) = frequency (Hz) × wavelength

so wavelength (m) = $\dfrac{\text{wave speed (m/s)}}{\text{frequency (Hz)}}$

$= \dfrac{3 \times 10^8}{107.6 \times 10^6}$

$= \dfrac{300\,000\,000}{107.6 \times 1\,000\,000}$

$= 2.79$ m

Remember: 1 MHz = 10^6 Hz or 1 000 000 Hz. You need to be able to carry out calculations where large numbers are written in so-called standard form.

Now try this

1. Explain why radio waves are the least harmful of all of the waves in the electromagnetic spectrum. **(2 marks)**

2. Identify the lowest frequency wave in the electromagnetic spectrum. **(1 mark)**

   A ☐ gamma rays   **B** ☐ X-rays   **C** ☐ radio waves   **D** ☐ ultraviolet waves

Microwaves

MICROWAVES are a type of radio wave, but they have a higher frequency than radio waves and so have slightly different properties.

Uses of microwaves

 Microwave ovens

In microwave ovens, water in the food absorbs the microwaves and turns this into thermal energy.

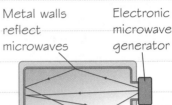

Metal walls reflect microwaves

Electronic microwave generator

Water in food absorbs microwaves

Microwaves transfer energy deep inside food

 Mobile phones

Phone 1

Microwave signal → Mast 1 (base station)

Signal transmitted along a cable

Phone 2

Microwave signal ← Mast 2 (base station)

 Satellite TV

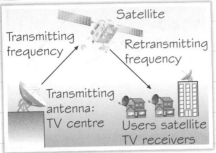

Satellite

Transmitting frequency

Retransmitting frequency

Transmitting antenna: TV centre

Users satellite TV receivers

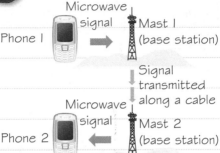 **Weather forecasting**

Weather forecasters use RADAR to locate rain.

 Communications

Communications to and from orbiting satellites (satellite phones on ships or aeroplanes, satellite television).

Characteristics

Microwaves have:
- a higher frequency than radio waves
- a shorter wavelength than radio waves.

Dangers of microwaves

When microwaves are absorbed by the body this can heat body tissue. Mobile phone radiation is at a very low intensity so the heating effect is minimal and normal exposure to microwaves from mobile phones has currently shown no harmful effects.

Worked example

(a) Describe **one** difference between radio waves and microwaves.
(1 mark)

Radio waves have a lower frequency compared to microwaves.

(b) Use your answer to explain why microwaves are potentially more harmful to living organisms than radio waves. **(2 marks)**

The higher the frequency of a wave, the more energy it has and the more harm it can do to living things. As microwaves have a higher frequency than radio waves, they are potentially more harmful compared to radio waves.

The frequency of a wave affects the potential to cause harm to an organism. The higher the frequency of the wave, the greater the potential to cause harm.

Now try this

1 Identify **two** uses of microwaves in the home. **(2 marks)**

2 Explain why microwave ovens have a shield to prevent microwaves escaping from them. **(2 marks)**

Infrared radiation

INFRARED RADIATION can be felt as heat but it cannot be seen. The hotter an object, the more infrared energy is given out. Most of the energy from the Sun that arrives on Earth is in the form of infrared radiation.

Cooking (grills, BBQ and toasters)

Thermal imaging and night vision equipment

Uses of infrared

Television remote controls (short infrared waves do not cause any heating)

Optical fibre communications (such as for cable TV and high-speed internet access)

Security systems that detect infrared energy from intruders

Characteristics

Infrared radiation has:

- a higher frequency and lower wavelength than radio waves or microwaves
- a higher wavelength than the red part of visible light (hence infrared).

Dangers of infrared radiation

Excessive exposure to infrared radiation can cause burning of the skin, such as when you get too close to a hot grill.

Remember: you don't have to be touching a hot object for it to burn you. Infrared radiation, like all electromagnetic radiation, can travel through a vacuum.

Worked example

Look at the image opposite from a security camera at night. Describe how infrared cameras allow the user to 'see' warm-blooded living organisms when there is no Sun or artificial light. **(2 marks)**

The infrared camera detects the infrared radiation given off by a living organism. All warm objects give off heat to their surroundings, so the camera is able to pick up on this heat and provide images of the organism.

Now try this

1 Identify **two** uses of infrared radiation. **(2 marks)**

2 Electromagnetic waves travel at the speed of light, 3×10^8 m/s. Calculate the wavelength of infrared radiation from the Sun that has a frequency of 2×10^{12} Hz. **(3 marks)**

3 Which type of electromagnetic wave has the highest frequency? **(1 mark)**

   A ☐ infrared   **B** ☐ radio waves   **C** ☐ visible light   **D** ☐ microwaves

Visible light

VISIBLE LIGHT is the only part of the electromagnetic spectrum that can be detected by the human eye. These waves are seen as all of the different colours of the rainbow and each of these colours has a slightly different wavelength.

Vision

Uses of visible light

Lighting up dark places

Visible light only travels in straight lines so you need to line up the receiver (your eye, or the camera) directly at the source of light

Characteristics

Visible light waves have:
• a higher frequency than infrared but a shorter wavelength
• a lower frequency but a longer wavelength than ultraviolet.

Dangers of visible light

Very bright light can damage the eyes, so it is important to never look directly at the Sun or into a laser beam.

Wavelength

The wavelengths increase through the following colours:
• **violet**   shortest wavelength
• **indigo**
• **blue**
• **green**
• **yellow**
• **orange**
• **red**   longest wavelength

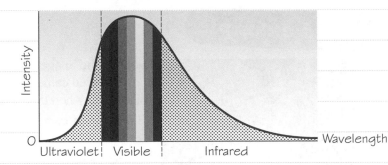

Worked example

Which colour of light has the shortest wavelength?   **(1 mark)**

A ☒ violet
B ☐ red
C ☐ green
D ☐ orange

Now try this

1 Which colour of light has the longest wavelength?   **(1 mark)**

A ☐ violet   B ☐ red
C ☐ green   D ☐ orange

2 Which **one** of the following is not a type of electromagnetic wave?   **(1 mark)**

A ☐ radio   B ☐ microwaves
C ☐ sound   D ☐ X-ray

Ultraviolet light

ULTRAVIOLET LIGHT is not visible to the human eye and is usually called UV light. Sunlight contains UV light – however the ozone layer blocks some of the UV light from the Sun reaching the Earth.

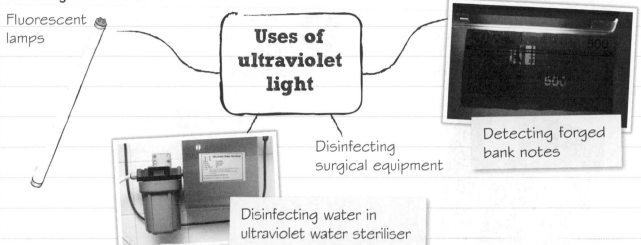

Fluorescent lamps

Uses of ultraviolet light

Disinfecting surgical equipment

Detecting forged bank notes

Disinfecting water in ultraviolet water steriliser

Characteristics

Ultraviolet light has:
• a shorter frequency than X-rays and a higher frequency than visible light
• a shorter wavelength than the violet part of visible light (hence ultraviolet).

Dangers of ultraviolet light

Too much ultraviolet light from the Sun damages cells at the surface of the skin and causes sunburn and also damage to the eyes such as cataracts and blindness. Damage to DNA in skin cells can eventually result in skin cancer.

The frequency of a wave affects the energy transferred from the wave. Higher frequency waves have more energy than lower frequency waves. Ultraviolet radiation has a higher frequency than visible light and so is more harmful.

Worked example

Explain why it is advisable for a person to put on sun cream and wear sunglasses when they go out in hot sunny climates.   **(3 marks)**

The Sun emits ultraviolet light. If the skin is exposed to too much UV light it will burn and can eventually lead to skin cancer. UV light can also damage the eyes so it is necessary to wear sunglasses that do not let UV light to pass through them to protect the eyes from UV damage.

Now try this

1 Explain why microwaves are less harmful than ultraviolet radiation.   **(2 marks)**

2 Electromagnetic waves travel at the speed of light, 3×10^8 m/s. Calculate the wavelength of ultraviolet waves from the Sun if the wave frequency is 1.2×10^{15} Hz.   **(3 marks)**

3 Identify **two** uses of UV light.   **(2 marks)**

X-rays

X-RAYS are emitted by stars and can also be generated for medical purposes.

Uses of X-rays

1 X-rays are used mainly in medicine to show teeth and bones. Bones and teeth absorb more X-rays than the skin, so they show up on the X-ray film as a white colour.

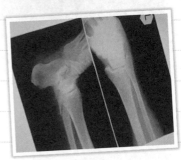

2 Airport security checks use X-rays to scan luggage to check for anything that may not be allowed to be carried onto a plane.

Characteristics

X-rays have:
- a higher frequency than ultraviolet light but less than gamma rays
- a shorter wavelength than ultraviolet light.

Dangers of X-rays

X-rays have very high frequencies and can cause mutations in DNA. This can kill cells or cause cancer.

A radiographer who takes X-rays in a hospital or a dentist wears a lead apron and stands behind a lead screen to protect them from exposure to X-rays.

Worked example

Explain why pregnant women are advised not to have medical X-rays. **(2 marks)**

X-rays can cause mutations in DNA. As a pregnant woman has a baby growing inside her, the X-rays may damage the DNA of the child and result in genetic mutations.

Now try this

1. Identify which wave has the highest frequency. **(1 mark)**

   A ☐ radio waves   **B** ☐ microwaves

   C ☐ ultraviolet rays   **D** ☐ X-rays

2. If an X-ray has a wavelength of 1.2×10^{-10} m and a frequency of 2.5×10^{18} Hz, calculate the wave speed of the X-ray. Show your working. **(2 marks)**

   wave speed (m/s) = frequency (Hz) × wavelength (m)

Gamma rays

GAMMA RAYS have the smallest wavelengths and the highest frequency compared to any other wave in the electromagnetic spectrum.

Uses of gamma rays

1 Detecting cancer

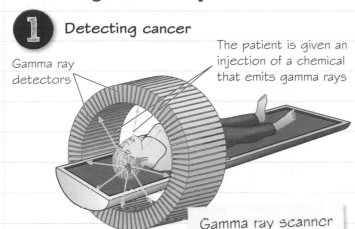

Gamma ray detectors

The patient is given an injection of a chemical that emits gamma rays

Gamma ray scanner

2 Cancer treatment

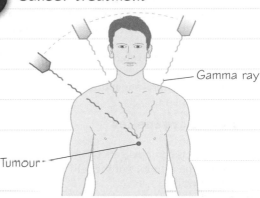

Gamma ray

Tumour

3 Sterilising food

4 Sterilising medical equipment

Gamma rays can kill living cells, which is why they are used to sterilise food and surgical instruments, but they can be carefully targeted and used in cancer treatment to destroy cancer cells.

Characteristics

Gamma rays have:
- an even higher frequency than X-rays
- an extremely short wavelength of less than 10 picometres.

10 picometres is less than the diameter of an atom!

Dangers of gamma rays

Exposure to gamma rays results in damage to DNA in cells in the body, which can kill the cells or cause different types of cancers.

CAUTION

Worked example

Explain why gamma rays can cause the most harm to humans compared to other waves in the electromagnetic spectrum. **(2 marks)**

Gamma rays have the highest frequency of all the waves in the electromagnetic spectrum, which means they have the highest energy. Having the highest energy means that they can cause more harm compared to other waves in the spectrum.

Now try this

1 Calculate the wave speed of a gamma ray with a wavelength of 2.0×10^{-12} m and a frequency of 1.5×10^{20} Hz. Show your working. **(2 marks)**

wave speed (m/s) = wavelength (m) × frequency (Hz)

 A negative power of ten gives the number of times the number has to be divided by 10.

69

Answers

Learning aim A

1. Cell structure and function 1
1 A
2 Motor neurones transmit electrical impulses from the central nervous system to muscles and organs.

2. Cell structure and function 2
1 A sperm cell's structure has a head that contains genetic material and the tail helps it swim to the egg. Its function is to fertilise an egg cell.
2 (a) Xylem transports water around the plant and also provides support.
   (b) Phloem transports sugars from the leaves around the rest of the plant.

3. Plant cell organelles
1 (a) The nucleus.
   (b) The nucleus contains genetic information that controls the activities of the cell.
   (c) The cell wall.
   (d) The cell wall provides shape and strength to the cell.

4. Animal cell organelles
1 C
2 B
3 Animal cells are usually an irregular shape because they do not have a rigid cell wall.

5. Cells, tissues and organs
1 A
2 C

6. Function of plant organs
1 (a) Xylem.
   (b) Phloem.

7. DNA
1 The nucleus.
2 DNA is a very long molecule made up of four different bases arranged in sequences on two strands. The four bases are adenine, thymine, guanine and cytosine. The base pairs link together in complimentary pairs to form a double helix.

8. Chromosomes and genes
1 Genes are made of DNA and give the instructions to a cell to tell it what to do.
2 Each chromosome carries thousands of different genes. Chromosomes come in pairs to make sure you inherit two copies of each gene – one from each parent.

9. Alleles, genotypes and phenotypes
1 Homozygous means that the two chromosomes in the sex cells have the same alleles for a certain gene.
2 A phenotype is a characteristic that is visible and does not change.

10. Punnett squares and pedigree diagrams
1

Parents	Mother	Father
Genotype	Gg	Gg
Phenotype	Grey	Grey
Gametes	G g	G g

Possible combinations

Genotype	GG	Gg	Gg	gg
Phenotype	Grey	Grey	Grey	White

2 A pedigree analysis diagram shows the inheritance of a phenotype in a family.

11. Predicting genetic outcomes
1 (a)

		Parent genotype	
	Parent gametes	D	d
Parent genotype	D	DD	Dd
	D	DD	Dd

   (b) There is no probability (0%) that the parents will have a child with this condition.
   (c) 100%

12. Genetic mutations
1

Base	A	T	C	G	C	C	A	T	A
Complementary base pair	T	A	G	C	G	G	T	A	T

2 If part of the base sequence on a DNA molecule is removed or changed, this results in changes in the genetic code which is called a mutation.

Learning aim B

13. Homeostasis
1 Homeostasis means keeping the same internal environment in the body. This is necessary so that the body's cells can function properly.
2 Body temperature and salt levels.

14. The nervous system
1 (a) Receptors detect stimuli.
   (b) Light receptors in the eyes and touch receptors in the skin.

15. Involuntary and voluntary responses
1 B
2 A voluntary response requires an organism to think about doing it before the action is performed. An involuntary response is much faster than a voluntary response because it does not require any thought processing by the CNS.

16. Synapses
1 An electrical impulse reaches the synapse at the end of the neurone. A chemical called a neurotransmitter is released into the gap and this causes a new electrical impulse in the next neurone.

17. Control of blood glucose
1 D
2 Hormones travel in the bloodstream.

18. Differences between the endocrine and nervous systems
1 C
2 The gland has to release the hormone into the bloodstream and then the blood has to carry the hormone to the target organ. This takes longer than the nervous system, which responds very quickly as the method of transport of the signal is much faster.

19. Thermoregulation

1 Vasoconstriction occurs, which takes blood away from the skin surface to reduce heat loss to the environment. She will also shiver, which is a muscle contraction causing an increase in body heat.

20. Learning aim B: 6-mark questions 1

This is an example answer. It is not the only correct answer.

1 The human body maintains a core temperature of 37°C as the chemical reactions in the body work best at this temperature. Core body temperature is maintained by homeostasis.

In cold conditions the body responds to maintain its heat and create heat by:

1 – raising body hair, which traps heat on the surface of the skin

2 – vasoconstriction of the blood vessels close to the skin. This means that these blood vessels narrow, which takes blood away from the skin surface and reduces heat loss to the environment

3 – shivering, when the muscles contract rapidly to cause an increase in body heat.

In hot conditions the body tries to lose heat in three main ways:

1 – lowering body hair which increases heat loss from the skin

2 – vasodilation of blood vessels close to the skin. This means that these blood vessels widen so that blood is brought closer to the skin surface, resulting in excess body heat being lost to the environment

3 – sweating, because the evaporation of sweat from the skin results in heat loss to the environment.

21. Learning aim B: 6-mark questions 2

This is an example answer. It is not the only correct answer.

1 The endocrine system is used mainly to maintain homeostasis, whereas the nervous system allows the body to respond instantly to a change in the environment. Both systems have effectors which produce responses. In the nervous system the effectors are muscles. They produce a movement in response to a nervous impulse. In the endocrine system, the effectors are glands which secrete a hormone, which in turn produces a response in the target organ. For example, the pancreas is a gland which secretes insulin when blood sugar levels are too high. The insulin targets the liver which responds by storing the excess blood sugar as glycogen.

The two systems transmit their information in very different ways. The nervous system has a much faster method of transferring information, which can take less than a second. The nervous system sends electrical impulses along nerve cells, and a chemical signal crosses the synapse to trigger the electrical impulse along the next neurone. In the endocrine system, it takes a much longer time for the response to occur. The gland releases a hormone which travels in the blood stream to the target organ, and the target organ then initiates a response. This all takes some time to occur. As a result, the effects of the endocrine system last much longer than the effects of the nervous system, as they can last minutes, hours or days. In comparison, the duration of a response in the nervous system is less than a second.

Learning aim C

22. The structure of an atom 1

1

Electrons	5
Protons	5
Neutrons	6

23. The structure of an atom 2

1 B

2 Outer shells.

3 Neutron.

24. Atomic number, mass number

1 8

2 12

3 (a) 4

(b) 4

(c) 5

25. The periodic table 1

1 Si

26. The periodic table 2

1 B

2 C

27. Isotopes and relative atomic mass

1 $$\frac{(6 \times 7.6) + (7 \times 92.4)}{100}$$

$$\frac{45.6 + 646.8}{100}$$

$$\frac{692.4}{100}$$

= 6.9

28. Filling electron shells 1

1 B

2 The second shell can hold 8 electrons and the third shell can also hold 8 electrons.

3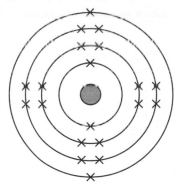

29. Filling electron shells 2

1 (a) 1

(b) 2.8.2

(c) 2.8.5

(d) 2.8.6

30. Electron shells and groups

1 (a) 2.8.3

(b) Group 3

2 Potassium and sodium are in the same group in the periodic table so they have the same number of electrons in their outer shells. This means that they have very similar chemical properties and will react with water in a similar way.

31. Metals and non-metals

1 Either Group 1 or Group 2

2 Either Group 7 or Group 8

ANSWERS

Learning aim D

32. Compounds and formulae
1 1 atom of copper, 1 atom of carbon, 3 atoms of oxygen.
2 B

33. Elements, compounds and mixtures
1 An element is made up of only one type of atom, whereas a compound is formed by two or more elements that have reacted and joined together.
2 B

34. Word equations
1 iron filings + sulfuric acid → iron sulfate + hydrogen

35. Balanced chemical equations
1 $Zn + 2HCl \rightarrow H_2 + ZnCl_2$
2 $CuO + H_2SO_4 \rightarrow H_2O + CuSO_4$

36. Acids, bases and alkalis
1 A
2 (a) Neutral.
   (b) It will turn red which means that it is a strong acid.

37. Neutralisation reactions
1 A
2 A salt and water.
3 Sodium hydroxide.

38. Equations for neutralisation reactions
1 C
2 sodium hydroxide + sulfuric acid → sodium sulfate + water

39. Reactions of acids with metals
1 Zinc chloride.
2

Name of metal	Name of acid		
	hydrochloric acid	nitric acid	sulfuric acid
aluminium	aluminium chloride	aluminium nitrate	aluminium sulfate
copper	no reaction	no reaction	no reaction
magnesium	magnesium chloride	magnesium nitrate	magnesium sulfate

40. Reactions of acids with carbonates
1 acid + metal carbonate → salt + carbon dioxide + water
2 sulfuric acid + copper carbonate → copper sulfate + water + carbon dioxide
3

Name of metal	Name of acid		
	hydrochloric acid	nitric acid	sulfuric acid
calcium carbonate	calcium chloride	calcium nitrate	calcium sulfate
copper carbonate	copper chloride	copper nitrate	copper sulfate
sodium carbonate	sodium chloride	sodium nitrate	sodium sulfate

41. Tests for hydrogen and carbon dioxide
1 (a) Limewater.
   (b) The limewater would go cloudy when the gas produced by the reaction was bubbled through it.

42. Hazard symbols
1 Moderate hazard.
2 A – 4 Environmental hazard.
   B – 3 Corrosive.
   C – 1 Toxic.
   D – 2 Flammable.

43. Applications of neutralisation reactions
1 Farmers use lime, which is a base, by adding it to acidic soil to neutralise some of the acid and so reduce the acidity.
2 A stomach produces hydrochloric acid to help digest your food. If too much hydrochloric acid is produced this can cause indigestion. Antacids can be taken as these are bases and so can help to neutralise the excess acid.

44. Learning aim D: 6-mark questions 1
This is an example answer. It is not the only correct answer.
1 The elements are arranged in the periodic table in order of increasing atomic number. The atomic number describes the number of protons in the nucleus, and therefore also the number of electrons around the nucleus. The arrangement of the electrons is called the electronic configuration.

There are 8 groups (vertical columns) in the periodic table.

There is a connection between the number of outer electrons an element has and the group in which it is positioned in the periodic table. Elements in the same group have the same number of electrons in their outer shells, so these elements all have very similar chemical properties.

Elements in Group 2 all have 2 electrons in their outer shell. The electronic configuration of some of the elements in Group 2 is shown in the table below.

Group 2	Atomic number	Electronic configuration
$_4^9Be$	4	2.2
$_{12}^{24}Mg$	12	2.8.2
$_{20}^{40}Ca$	20	2.8.8.2

45. Learning aim D: 6-mark questions 2
This is an example answer. It is not the only correct answer.
1 The equation for the reaction between hydrochloric acid and sodium carbonate is shown below:

$2HCl + Na_2CO_3 \rightarrow 2NaCl + CO_2 + H_2O$

hydrochloric acid + sodium carbonate → sodium chloride + carbon dioxide + water

To test that carbon dioxide has been produced, Gary would need to bubble the gas produced through limewater. To do this, he would need limewater, two test tubes, a bung and a tube as shown in the diagram below:

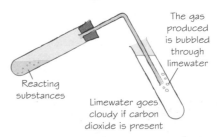

The gas produced is bubbled through limewater

Reacting substances

Limewater goes cloudy if carbon dioxide is present

The equation for the reaction between iron and sulfuric acid is shown below:
iron + sulfuric acid → iron sulfate + hydrogen
$Fe + H_2SO_4 \rightarrow FeSO_4 + H_2$

72

To test for hydrogen, Gary will need a test tube to collect the gas produced and a wooden splint. The wooden splint is lit and is put close to the mouth of the test tube that contains the gas. If hydrogen is present, there will be a popping sound. This occurs because the flame from the wooden splint lights the hydrogen, making it burn explosively and producing the popping noise.

46. Balanced equations for reactions with acids
1 (a) $2HCl + CaCO_3 \rightarrow CaCl_2 + H_2O + CO_2$
   (b) $ZnO + 2HNO_3 \rightarrow Zn(NO_3)_2 + H_2O$
   (c) $H_2SO_4 + 2NaOH \rightarrow 2H_2O + Na_2SO_4$

Learning aim E

47. Forms of energy
1 B
2 Light energy and thermal energy.

48. Uses of energy
1 As central heating and to heat water.
2

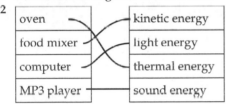

oven	kinetic energy
food mixer	light energy
computer	thermal energy
MP3 player	sound energy

49. Energy stores
1 Stored chemical energy is transformed initially into thermal, sound and light energy as the fuel is combusted. This is followed by kinetic energy as the rocket moves upwards.
2 Food, batteries and fuel cells.
3 A drawn bow and a trampoline when a person lands on it.
4 When the child lands on the trampoline the springs of the trampoline gain elastic potential energy. This energy is then transferred back to the child as kinetic energy so propelling them upwards from the trampoline. At the top of their bounce, they have gravitational potential energy as the energy is stored in the child because of their position.

50. Thermal energy transfers
1 Radiation.
2 Convection transfers thermal energy in a liquid or gas such as water or air. The thermal energy heats the fluid making it less dense and causing it to rise. Cooler, more dense fluid then replaces it and so a convection current has been set up, moving energy between the hot and cool parts of the fluid.

51. Measuring energy
1 A
2 The total amount of energy before an energy transfer is always the same as the total amount of energy afterwards.

52. Power
1 Power = energy / time
        = 9000 / 180
        = 50W

2 Power is how quickly a machine can transfer energy per second. This can be worked out by dividing the amount of energy the machine uses in joules divided by the time in seconds.

53. Paying for electricity
1 (a) Cost of electricity = number of kWhr × cost per unit
                           = 1 × 10
                           = 10p
   (b) Cost of electricity = number of kWhr × cost per unit
                           = (5 × 2) × 10
                           = £1.00
   (c) Cost of electricity = number of kWhr × cost per unit
                           = (0.1 × 0.5) × 10
                           = 0.5p

54. Efficiency of energy transfers
1 (a) Light bulb A = 60/80 × 100 = 75%
   (b) Light bulb B = 30/80 × 100 = 37.5%
2 Light bulb A is much more efficient compared to light bulb B. Light bulb A transfers 75% of the total energy supplied into light energy, with only 25% of the energy being wasted as thermal energy. Light bulb B is only 37.5% efficient, so only 37.5% of the energy put into the light bulb is transferred to light energy and 62.5% of the energy transferred is wasted energy.

55. Renewable energy resources
1 (a) Solar energy and tidal energy.
   (b) Wind turbines transform kinetic energy of the wind directly into electrical energy by using the wind to turn a turbine.

56. Non-renewable energy resources
1 C
2 Coal and gas.

57. Using energy effectively
1 Electrical energy is transferred into thermal energy in many homes. Therefore by using double glazing or loft insulation less thermal energy is lost and wasted. Turning all electrical appliances off rather than leaving them on standby will reduce the use of electrical energy in the home.
2 Generating electricity causes pollution and uses up non-renewable energy resources, so it is important to conserve these for as long as possible.

58. Learning aim E: 6-mark questions 1
This is an example answer. It is not the only correct answer.
1 The car engine burns petrol. Petrol is a form of chemical energy, and when it is burned it transforms this energy into mechanical energy. This mechanical energy is used to turn the wheels of the car, making the car move, so the mechanical energy is transformed into kinetic energy. The process of the petrol being burned will also be transferred into thermal energy, and the moving parts in the engine and the rest of the car produce sound, so the chemical energy is also transformed into sound energy.

This transformation of chemical energy into sound and thermal energy is wasted energy, as the main purpose of the chemical energy is to be transformed into mechanical and then kinetic energy. This means that the transformation is not 100% efficient. This is the case with all energy transformations – some energy is always wasted as it is transformed into types of energy that are not required for the main purpose of the energy transformation.

59. Learning aim E: 6-mark questions 2

This is an example answer. It is not the only correct answer.

1 The archer eats food which is chemical energy and their body stores this chemical energy. Chemical energy is transformed into mechanical energy to move the muscles of the body, and this mechanical energy is transformed into kinetic energy as the archer moves to place the arrow in the correct place and draw the bow.

The kinetic energy is then transformed into stored elastic potential energy as the bow is stretched, storing this energy. When the archer lets go of the bow, the stored elastic potential energy is then transformed into kinetic energy as the arrow moves through the air towards the target. When the arrow hits the target, some of the kinetic energy is transferred into sound energy, as a noise is made when the arrow hits the target, and some will be transferred into thermal energy.

Learning aim F

60. Wave characteristics

1

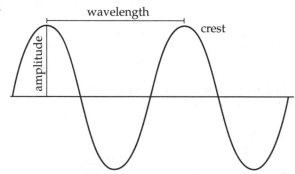

2 (a) m
(b) m/s
(c) Hz
(d) m

61. Wave calculations

1 wave speed = frequency × wavelength
$$= 100 \times 10$$
$$= 1000 \, \text{m/s}$$

2 frequency = wave speed / wavelength
$$= 100 / 5$$
$$= 20 \, \text{Hz}$$

62. The electromagnetic spectrum

1 B
2 C

63. Radio waves

1 The higher the frequency the wave the more energy the wave transfers, therefore the more harm the wave can do to human health. As radio waves have the lowest frequency they are the least harmful of all of the waves in the electromagnetic spectrum.

2 C

64. Microwaves

1 Satellite TV and mobile phones.

2 When microwaves are absorbed by the body this can heat body tissue. This is why microwave ovens have shields to prevent the microwaves from escaping and harming people.

65. Infrared radiation

1 Cooking and thermal imaging.

2 wavelength = wave speed / frequency
$$= 3 \times 10^8 / 2 \times 10^{12}$$
$$= 1.5 \times 10^{-4} \, \text{m} = 0.00015 \, \text{m}$$

3 C

66. Visible light

1 B
2 C

67. Ultraviolet light

1 Microwaves have a lower frequency than ultraviolet radiation, therefore it is less harmful.

2 wavelength = wave speed / frequency
$$= 3 \times 10^8 / 1.2 \times 10^{15}$$
$$= 2.5 \times 10^{-7} \, \text{m}$$

3 Disinfecting water and fluorescent lamps.

68. X-rays

1 D

2 wave speed (m/s) = frequency (Hz) × wavelength (m)
$$= (2.5 \times 10^{18}) \times (1.2 \times 10^{-10})$$
$$= 3 \times 10^8 \, \text{m/s}$$

69. Gamma rays

1 wave speed (m/s) = wavelength (m) × frequency (Hz)
$$= (1.5 \times 10^{20}) \times (2.0 \times 10^{-12})$$
$$= 3 \times 10^8 \, \text{m/s}$$

Your own notes

Your own notes

Your own notes

Published by Pearson Education Limited, Edinburgh Gate, Harlow, Essex, CM20 2JE.

www.pearsonschoolsandfecolleges.co.uk

Copies of official specifications for all BTEC qualifications may be found on the Edexcel website: www.edexcel.com

Text © Pearson Education Limited 2013
Edited, produced and typeset by Wearset Ltd, Boldon, Tyne and Wear
Original illustrations © Pearson Education Limited 2013
Illustrated by Wearset Ltd, Boldon, Tyne and Wear
Cover illustration by Miriam Sturdee

First published 2013

17 16 15 14 13
10 9 8 7 6 5 4 3

British Library Cataloguing in Publication Data
A catalogue record for this book is available from the British Library

ISBN 978 1 446 90277 6

Printed in Slovakia by Neografia

Acknowledgements
The author and publisher would like to thank the following individuals and organisations for their kind permission to reproduce photographs:

(Key: b-bottom; c-centre; l-left; r-right; t-top)

Alamy Images: Ingram Publishing 69, Jason Cox 31r, Phil Degginger 30r; **Digital Stock:** 12r; **Digital Vision:** 48bl; **Fotolia.com:** Dirk Hoffmann 31l; **Getty Images:** Eco Images 43cr; **Imagemore Co., Ltd:** 68tl; **Pearson Education Ltd:** Gareth Boden 30l, 39, 40, Joey Chan 33l, Coleman Yuen 67tl, 67tr, Richard Smith 68cr, Sozaijiten 48cl, Trevor Clifford 33tc, 33tr, 33cr, 41, 57tl; **PhotoDisc:** Doug 43cl, H. Wiesenhofer. Photolink. 66tc; **Photolibrary.com:** Stockbyte. George Doyle. 55tr, 58cr; **Science Photo Library Ltd:** 68c, Claire Deprez / Reporters 43tl, G. Brad Lewis 55bl, Martin Bond 57r, T-Service 65; **Shutterstock.com:** Gerald Bernard 43tr, Helder Almeida 13tl, 18, maigi 48cr; **Veer/Corbis:** Andreas Karelias 53tc, dgmata 53tl, eyeidea 53tr, godrick 9, Olena Mykhaylova 55tl, 58cl, Pelagic 12l, Rigamondis 55cl, stefano lunardi 8, 66, uulgaa 48tl, Wavebreakmediamicro 45; **www.imagesource.com:** 66tl, Amy Eckert 19

All other images © Pearson Education

Picture research by: Caitlin Swain

Every effort has been made to contact copyright holders of material reproduced in this book. Any omissions will be rectified in subsequent printings if notice is given to the publishers.

In the writing of this book, no BTEC examiners authored sections relevant to examination papers for which they have responsibility.